MARIETTA D. MOSKIN

Sky Dragons and Flaming Swords

The Story of Eclipses, Comets, and Other Strange Happenings in the Skies

Walker and Company • New York, New York

Acknowledgments

I would like to give thanks to Professor Lloyd Motz of Columbia University for checking my manuscript for scientific accuracy. My thanks and appreciation also to Marcy Pedas Sigler for sparking my interest in this subject and for supplying me with large amounts of research material and technical advice.

M. M.

First published in the United States of America in 1985 by the Walker Publishing Company, Inc.

Published simultaneously in Canada by John Wiley & Sons Canada, Limited, Rexdale, Ontario.

Library of Congress Cataloging in Publication Data

Moskin, Marietta D.
  Sky dragons and flaming swords.

  Bibliography: p.
  Includes index.
  Summary: Discusses unusual sky phenomena and how they affected our earliest ancestors, giving rise to superstitions and myths.
    1. Astronomy—Juvenile literature. 2. Eclipses—Juvenile literature. 3. Comets—Juvenile literature. 4. Meteors—Juvenile literature. 5. Astronomy—Folklore—Juvenile literature. [1. Astronomy—History]
  I. Title.
  QB46.M87 1985   520   84–22206
  ISBN 0–8027–6574–2
  ISBN 0–8027–6575–0 (lib. bdg.)

Printed in the United States of America

10 9 8 7 6 5 4 3 2

Contents

Introduction

We live in an ordered universe. The stars, planets, and satellites that we see in the night sky move in predictable orbits. Although their positions differ from season to season and from hour to hour, these changes form familiar patterns.

Our earliest ancestors, who lived without clocks or calendars, knew from these recurring patterns of the sun, moon, and stars when to plant and harvest their crops, when to hunt the young deer or gather berries in the spring, when to start putting away food for the long winter. And this continuing sameness signaled to them that all was well in the heavens and on the earth.

Sometimes, though, there were unusual movements in the sky. The sun or moon might suddenly vanish, or intruding lights would trace new and strange patterns among familiar constellations. These events were frightening to people who did not understand the causes. Until fairly recent times, in fact, people panicked when they saw solar or lunar eclipses, comets, or meteors. They often thought the end of the world was coming, and they didn't know what to do. Even today, primitive people living in remote areas react with fear and superstition to changes in the sky.

This book tells the story of how these unusual but predictable "sky shows" have been "explained" in myths and legends, and how they have contributed valuable information about the universe in which we live.

Chapter 1

Signs and Signals

The battle was at its height. Sword clashed against sword, spear crashed against battle axe. Foot soldiers, their bows drawn, hurled iron-tipped arrows towards their foes. Dust rose as horses charged and camels trampled the earth. Amidst it all, shields and breastplates flashed like jewels in the morning sun.

It was May 28, 585 B.C. The war between the Lydians and the Medes—begun over a petty quarrel—had surged for six long years backward and forward over the barren lands of what is today Turkey. Now the old enemies had met again, this time on the banks of the River Halys, which marked the boundary between their lands. Each side was sure that it would emerge victorious at last.

But neither side would yield. Blood stained the earth and tinged the river as it flowed north toward the far-off shores of the Black Sea. The screams of dying men and wounded horses filled the air.

And then, though the sky was cloudless and the day had barely begun, darkness crept over the battlefield. At first, hardly anyone noticed the change in the light. But finally it could not be overlooked. Astonished, all the warriors, Lydian and Mede alike, looked up into the sky. A shadow moved across the sun. Moment by moment, the day grew darker. . . .

A hush fell over the battlefield. This was an omen, without doubt! Why were the gods displeased? And which side bore the blame? There was no way to tell.

Lydians and Medes flee in panic when a total eclipse of the sun interrupts their battle in 585 B.C.

Lydians and Medes put down their arms and fled to their own lines as the untimely "night" grew darker. This was not a matter for simple soldiers to decide. This strange event was for oracles, magicians, and soothsayers to study and interpret.

Slowly the threatening shadow moved away and the returning sun shone brightly on the dead and dying left behind. The day was as before, but the battle did not resume. The gods had spoken.

Within days, go-betweens approached King Cyaxares of the Medes and King Alyattes of Lydia and proposed terms to end the war. The settlement involved the taking of oaths, solemnized by the mingling of blood drawn from the arm of each opponent. And, to make sure the peace would last, a marriage was arranged between the Lydian princess, Aryenis, and Asyages, the son of Cyaxares.

And so, after those six long years of war, peace came to the Lydians and the Medes.

• • •

Today we know that the strange shadow across the sun that ended the war between the Lydians and the Medes was caused not by a wrathful god but by an ordinary natural phenomenon: a solar eclipse.

An eclipse occurs when one heavenly body passes into the shadow of another. For instance, during a solar eclipse, the earth, the moon, and the sun line up in such a way that the moon passes between the sun and the earth, thus blotting out the light from the sun for a short period. Total darkness rarely lasts longer than four or five minutes, but some of the effects of the eclipse can be observed for an hour or so as the shadow of the moon slowly advances and then retreats across the earth.

Solar eclipses are not really rare. During each century, about sixty-six total eclipses happen, and two hundred or more partial eclipses can be observed. Eclipses seem unusual because a total eclipse is visible only within a narrow path of a hundred miles or so. And while eclipses occur in regular cycles, one can see a total eclipse from any particular spot on earth only once every 360 years.

For people of ancient cultures, the chances of seeing an eclipse, or even hearing of one, were certainly slim. It was no wonder that they panicked when the normally reliable sun vanished from their sky.

To our earliest ancestors, the sun was more than just a light. It was a life-giving heavenly force. They dimly understood that without the sun, life would not be possible on the earth. For this reason, many cultures worshiped the sun and moon as gods. Others believed that specific gods moved these great lights across the dome-shaped heavenly vault, which sheltered the flat earth below.

People who pictured the earth as flat and the sky as a domed "ceiling" could not possibly have understood how eclipses really work. Even the most learned people of the ancient world did not understand that our sun is a star, that the stars visible in the night sky are millions of different "suns" seen from a vast distance, and that all of these heavenly bodies, including our earth, are huge spinning balls of rock and gas, circling around each other and traveling through space.

And yet, at a remarkably early stage in human history, some sky watchers knew a great deal about the movements of stars and planets. Because the sun was so important to life on earth, early astronomers in all parts of the world kept careful records about movements in the skies—unusual ones as well as those that happen regularly. Eclipses of the moon and sun were unusual events. So were sightings of comets and meteors. All of these strange happenings were regarded as important omens— signs from the gods that had to be interpreted and obeyed.

The ancient Babylonians were among the earliest watchers of the skies, and their astronomers observed that solar eclipses repeated themselves every eighteen years, occurring each time about 120 degrees farther west on the surface of the earth. The Babylonians called each of those eighteen-year cycles a Saros. It takes three Saros cycles (fifty-four years and one month, to be exact) for an eclipse to reoccur at the same longitude.

The Chaldeans, who conquered the Babylonians about two thousand years later, refined some of the Babylonian calculations through careful observations recorded over many centuries. They discovered that the sequence of eclipses of the sun and moon is repeated every 6,585 days, or every 223 lunar months, which are measured from one new moon to the next.

During that same period, sky watchers in ancient China were also making precise observations. Perhaps the earliest mention of an eclipse occurs in a Chinese document called the *Shu Ching*, which records that "the sun and the moon did not meet harmoniously," possibly referring to the eclipse of October 22, 2134 B.C. Legends tell that the two royal astronomers

Hsi and Ho failed to predict the event and were beheaded for their negligence. Since the emperor, like his people, believed that eclipses were caused by an invisible dragon devouring the sun, it was crucial to be warned in time so that he could summon his drummers and archers, whose noise and arrows would frighten away the dragon. That day, he was not warned, and even though the light of the sun did return, the emperor was merciless to his careless astronomers. Being a royal astronomer in ancient China was a dangerous job.

Chinese priests, like many others elsewhere, regarded eclipses as miraculous events that had to be interpreted as omens. They would carve descriptions of eclipses on "oracle bones" (or "dragon bones")—small pieces of tortoiseshell or animal bones, which were then heated to produce cracks. The priests would then "read" these cracks to help find answers to their questions about the omen.

One oracle bone found in northeast China provides a very early description of an eclipse: "Three flames ate the sun, and a great star was seen." But while mention of eclipses on dragon bones is intriguing, modern astronomers find it difficult to assign specific dates to most of them since the Chinese method of calculating time was so different.

One sighting recorded at Ugarith, in northwest Syria, can be dated with more precision. A clay tablet found at that site tells us that "the day of the new moon in the month of Hiyar [April–May] was put to shame. The sun went down in the daytime with Rashap [Mars] in attendance. This means the overlord will be attacked by his vassals." This was probably the eclipse of May 3, 1375 B.C., which was visible from that location.

Another ancient eclipse that can be dated rather precisely is mentioned in early Assyrian records. The text reads: "Insurrection in the City of Ashur. In the month of Sivan, the sun was eclipsed. . . ." Modern astronomers believe this was the eclipse of June 15, 763 B.C.

This eclipse is also mentioned in the Bible, in a passage of the Old Testament where the Hebrew prophet Amos tells of one of his visions: ". . . and on that day, says the Lord God, I will make the sun go down at noon, and darken the Earth in broad daylight . . ." (Amos 8:9). Amos, who prophesied between 765 and 750 B.C., may have seen the eclipse himself or been told about it.

There are also many reports of eclipses in the writings of early Greek philosophers and historians. The historian Herodotus, who wrote about the battle between the Lydians and the Medes, understood that eclipses are not isolated events unrelated to ordinary astronomical patterns. In fact, he describes another one in his *History*, this one during the war between the Persians and the Greeks. Once again, everyone concerned, including Herodotus himself, accepted the disappearance of the sun as a heavenly omen. Xerxes, the Persian king, consulted his magicians, who advised him that the omen predicted destruction for the Greeks, since "the sun foretells for them, and the moon for us."

Reassured, Xerxes proceeded. In the short run, he piled up victories against the Greeks, but within a year he was soundly defeated. (Interpreting eclipses in terms of omens can be a risky business.)

Herodotus believed that the eclipse during the battle of the River Halys had earlier been predicted by the Greek philosopher Thales. Herodotus lived about a century after the battle, Thales nearly a century before it. Modern astronomers doubt that Thales could have had enough information to calculate an eclipse for a particular time and place more than one hundred years into the future. Although Thales was probably well acquainted with the Babylonian Saros cycles, it's difficult to estimate how much he really knew.

There were early astronomers in the western hemisphere, too. Mayan priests in ancient Mexico kept careful records of heavenly events over many centuries. Among those that were not destroyed, one predicts the dates when either the sun or the moon might suddenly vanish from the sky. The numbers closely resemble those of the Chaldean Saros cycles.

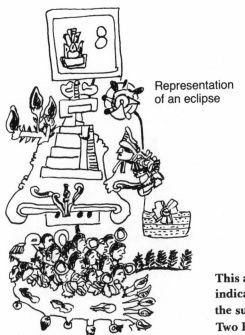

Representation
of an eclipse

**This ancient Mexican record
indicates that an eclipse of
the sun occurred in the year
Two Reed (1507).**

Druid priests, who practiced their religion in England as long as 3,900 years ago, are said to have had great knowledge about the movements of stars and planets. The ruins of the ancient circular monument called Stonehenge date from that time. This monument consists of huge upright slabs of stone forming circles within circles. Originally, the outer circle was capped by equally huge stone slabs placed across the tops of the columns. Some people believe that Stonehenge was used as an astronomical observatory and also as a primitive "computer" to predict eclipses. This idea arose when modern scientists noticed that certain eclipses are always visible between certain stones, and that the number of years between eclipses corresponds to a circle of post holes, called Aubrey Holes, that ring the outer stone circle.

While it is certain that the druids worshiped the sun and the moon and may well have studied their movements, it is doubtful that they kept the careful, long-term records needed for predicting eclipses.

Chapter 2

Space Dragons and Other Fancies

The Greek word *eclipse* means "forsaking" or "abandonment," and that is how the ancient Greeks regarded the occasions when either the sun or the moon suddenly seemed to vanish. The sun or the moon had abandoned them, and they were scared. The Greek poet Homer may have been the first person to use the word "eclipse" to describe the disappearance of the sun or the moon. Later, it was also used in that sense by the Greek historian Herodotus.

Not all the ancient priests, magicians, and early astronomers believed that the great lights in the sky had abandoned them, for many of them knew that eclipses occur in cycles. But they did not understand the true nature of these events either. In any case, they did not share their knowledge with the common folk—and this secrecy is understandable. Knowledge is a kind of power, and the ability to predict an eclipse added to the stature of a royal soothsayer or magician. And if members of the royal court also believed that these astronomers had special powers, so much the better. This was true throughout the ancient world, in China, Babylonia, Greece, and Mexico.

Mark Twain's story *A Connecticut Yankee in King Arthur's Court* shows just how impressive such knowledge could be. In Twain's story, a young man, Hank Morgan, is magically transported from nineteenth-century America to sixth-century England. Finding himself in prison and condemned to be burned at the stake, Hank takes heart when he remembers that an eclipse of the sun is due to occur over King Arthur's castle on the very day and hour of his scheduled execution.

Hank Morgan sends a message to King Arthur saying, "Tell the King that at that hour I will smother the whole world in the dead and blackness of midnight; I will blot out the sun, and he shall never shine again; the fruits of the earth shall rot for lack of light and warmth and the peoples of the earth shall famish and die, to the last man!"

It is a powerful warning, but the king is doubtful and orders the execution to proceed. And despite his brave words, Hank Morgan isn't really sure his ruse will work until, with the fire almost lit, people begin to stare at the sky.

"I followed their eyes; as sure as guns, there was my eclipse beginning! The life went boiling through my veins; I was a new man! The rim of black spread slowly into the sun's disk, my heart beat higher and higher, and still the assemblage and the priest stared into the sky, motionless. I knew that this gaze would be turned upon me, next. When it was, I was ready. I was in one of the most grand attitudes I ever struck, with my arm stretched up pointing to the sun. It was a noble effect."

Then it was King Arthur's turn to be afraid. "Name any terms, revered sir, even to the halving of my kingdom; but banish this calamity, spare the sun!"

But Hank Morgan's troubles were not over: "My fortune was made. I would have to take him up in a minute, but *I* couldn't stop an eclipse; the thing was out of question. So I asked time to consider."

The moments passed. Hank Morgan went on stalling desperately, while "it got pitch dark, at last, and the multitude groaned with horror to feel the cold uncanny night breezes fan through the place and see the stars come out and twinkle in the sky. At last the eclipse was total, and I was very glad of it, but everyone else was in misery; which was quite natural."

Lifting his hands, Hank intoned: "Let the enchantment dissolve and pass harmlessly away!"

A moment or two later, "the silver rim of the sun pushed

itself out," and Hank Morgan, the Connecticut Yankee, became the most important magician at King Arthur's court.

Mark Twain's story is fiction, and he got the dates wrong—there was no solar eclipse over England on June 21, 528—but he provides a clear picture of how people in medieval England might have reacted to someone able to predict an eclipse with such accuracy.

Mark Twain's hero, in fact, gets the idea of how to save himself from a real-life example. He remembers that Christopher Columbus used his knowledge of lunar eclipses to save himself and his shipmates from starvation.

This story was recounted in a journal kept by thirteen-year-old Ferdinand Columbus, who accompanied his father on his fourth voyage to America in 1503. Marooned for a year on the island of Jamaica while his ships were being repaired, Columbus depended on local Indians to furnish him and his crew with food. At first the Indians were friendly, but suddenly one day they refused to bring more food. Columbus needed a strong means of persuasion. He found it when he read in his ship's almanac that there would be a total eclipse of the moon on February 29, 1504.

Columbus threatened the Indians that he would extinguish the light of the moon if they would not bring him the corn, fish, and cassava root he needed. At first the Indians refused. But that night, when the shadow of the earth moved across the face of the moon, they changed their minds. Crying with fear, they came running, begging Columbus to bring back the moon. Columbus promised he would confer with God—to see if the Indians might be forgiven. And he seemed to be communicating with God as he sat silently, gazing at the hourglass with which he was timing the eclipse.

Just before the end of totality, Columbus announced that God had forgiven the Indians and would permit the moon to return to its place in the sky.

For the rest of their stay in Jamaica, Columbus and his men had plenty to eat.

Christopher Columbus used his knowledge of lunar eclipses to impress frightened Indians on the island of Jamaica in 1504.

In these two examples, one fictional and one true, human beings claiming special powers seem to make the sun or moon disappear. That is one type of superstition. There are many others connected with eclipses that were, and still are, believed in different parts of the world.

According to one type of superstition, the sun and moon possess human feelings, emotions, and weaknesses. For example, the Ainu people of Japan believe that an eclipse is a sign that the sun (or the moon) is sick, fainting, or dying. After all, they say, the sun turns black in the face!

To revive the dying god, the Ainu shake drops of water toward the sun with their "god-sticks." The Ainu, a Caucasian people, are said to be the oldest inhabitants of the Japanese islands. Their forebears are thought to have lived in that part of the world over six thousand years. No doubt their ideas about eclipses reflect fears common among our earliest human ancestors. Similar beliefs are still held by certain American In-

An example of noisemaking to frighten away evil spirits: Turks firing guns in Constantinople during the lunar eclipse of 1877 . . . the same eclipse that frightened Laotians halfway around the world.

dian tribes, by the Hottentots of Africa, and by some primitive peoples on the Indonesian island of Sumatra.

Some inhabitants of the northernmost parts of our globe have a different interpretation of what happens during an eclipse. They believe that the missing sun (or moon) has left the sky temporarily in order to check up on the people living on earth. The Alaskan Indians, Eskimos, Aleuts, and Tlingits all share this belief.

Another widespread belief is that during an eclipse the sun or moon is gradually being eaten by a terrifying monster in the sky. Bite by bite, the glowing disk grows smaller. The nature of the monster varies. In China and ancient Thailand, it is a dragon. In many parts of Africa and also in Indonesia, the monster nibbling at the sun is a snake. In much of South America, it is a jaguar. The ancient Germanic tribes of northern Eu-

Peruvian Indians use drums and noisemakers to disperse the shadow across the sun during an eclipse in the early 1800s.

rope accused hounds, coyotes, or wolves. (Those were the animals most plentiful and mischievous in their world.) In India, the imaginary culprits are the star monsters Rāhu and Ketu.

Whether the culprit is a monster, a dragon, a snake, or a wolf, the remedy is the same—to make as much noise as possible during eclipses to chase away the thieving beast. Making noise includes chanting, shouting, beating on drums, sticks, or, in modern times, pots and pans.

Another way of interpreting an eclipse is to see it as a battle between the sun and the moon. This superstition comes a little closer to reality, because it recognizes that an eclipse is caused by the *interaction* of the sun and the moon.

In the African state of Dahomey, the fight is between the sun god, Lisa, and the goddess of the moon, Gliti. Almost halfway around the world, on the northeast coast of South America, Indians in Surinam share a similar belief—that an eclipse is a fight between older brother Sun and younger brother Moon. It is a dangerous battle, for if the sun fails to win, the world will be doomed to everlasting night.

15

Besides making a lot of noise to stop the fight, many people daub themselves with thick white clay, perhaps to brighten the darkness caused by the eclipse. The traditions include a cleansing rite to wash away the blood shed by the wounded moon.

During the recent eclipse of June 20, 1973, several teams of scientists studied the reactions of people in Africa and South America. They were surprised at the similarity of traditions in places so far away from each other. Since solar eclipses happen so seldom in any one locality, the existence of regular eclipse traditions is in itself surprising.

The existence of a tradition doesn't necessarily mean that the "protection remedies" are still carried out today, however. Village elders in modern Surinam complained when young people refused to provide noise or participate in other eclipse rituals. In frustration, a group of old women, long after the eclipse had passed, dipped palm leaves in thick white clay and daubed villagers with it—often over vehement protests. But their efforts meant that the last step in the ritual would be carried out—a dip in the nearby river!

The scientists noted differences in tradition, too. Ethiopian tribesmen chewed and spat out medicinal aloe leaves to help cure the wounded sun. In Moslem regions, eclipse remedies involved a great deal of wailing and weeping and praying to Allah—a mixture of old superstitions and modern religious beliefs.

While Africans and South American Indians think of eclipses as battles between the sun and the moon, the gentle, peaceful natives of Tahiti believe an eclipse occurs when the sun and the moon are making love.

And some primitive peoples who watched scientists set up observation points and pass overhead in helicopters have blamed the scientists for stealing away their sun!

Space monsters? Battles in the sky? Omens and warnings from the gods? A sick or dying god? For thousands of years, people have tried to find out why the dependable movements

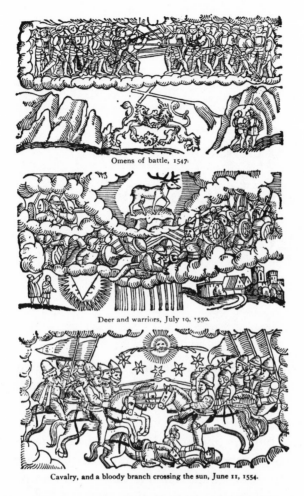

Omens of battle, 1547.

Deer and warriors, July 19, 1550.

Cavalry, and a bloody branch crossing the sun, June 11, 1554.

Our forefathers thought of sinister omens and bloody battles whenever they noted any strange movements or lights in the skies.

of the sun and moon have been disrupted from time to time. The stories they have invented to explain these events were influenced by their geography, their natural surroundings, their myths and religious beliefs, and of course by their image of the universe.

Not until pioneering astronomers mapped out the relationship between stars, planets, and other heavenly bodies could people begin to understand the mechanical nature of the predictable events that had previously caused such fear.

Chapter 3

Eclipses: The Facts and Figures

Today we know that neither the sun nor the moon actually disappears during an eclipse. But to understand what happens, it is important to know something about the movements of the sun, the moon, and the earth.

All the billions of stars, planets, and satellites in our universe are constantly in motion as they drift in space. Planets circle around stars, smaller satellites circle around planets, and all of these objects also spin on their own axis, each one at its own speed. A busy place! Luckily, the distances are vast, so the danger of collision is minimal. Besides, each is held to its own particular elliptical path (or orbit) by the force of gravity and by the speed at which it travels.

Our own small corner in the endless reaches of the universe is called the solar system. It consists of a group of nine related planets circling around the star we call the sun. The oval-shaped orbits of these planets differ in shape and size based on their distances from the sun. Each one travels at a different speed as well. Our planet, Earth, makes one complete orbit (its path around the sun) approximately every 365 days.

ECLIPSES: THE FACTS AND FIGURES

The length of an Earth day is determined by the time it takes our planet to spin around its own axis. Within the space of a twenty-four-hour day, each part of the earth faces the sun about half of the time and away from the sun the other half. When our particular spot on Earth faces away from the sun, we experience darkness and night.

While the earth rolls along on its journey around the sun, the moon circles the earth in a similar way, taking a little more than 27 days to complete its orbit. (But because the earth is moving at the same time, the moon takes 29 days, 12 hours, 44 minutes and 2.8 seconds for us to see all the different phases.)

We can see the moon when the side visible from the earth is illumined by the bright rays of the sun. This happens during the part of the month when the moon travels *away* from the sun, around the far side of the earth (Fig. 1). Each day we can see a little more of the moon, until the side that is permanently turned toward Earth is fully illuminated. We call that phase the *full moon*.

On the other hand, when the moon reaches the position where sunlight strikes only the side facing away from Earth, we can't see the moon at all. That phase is called the *new moon*. Between those two points, increasing (waxing) and decreasing (waning) slices of illuminated moon can be seen from earth at different times. Occasionally, even the rest of the moon is visible because of earthshine, which is sunlight reflected from the earth to the moon.

An eclipse of the moon occurs when, at full moon, the sun, the earth, and the moon are lined up in such a way that the earth prevents the rays of the sun from reaching the surface of the much smaller moon. At that time, the moon must travel through a band of Earth's shadow, called the umbra, until it can reach sunlight once again (Fig. 2). The time it takes the moon to move through the umbra varies from under an hour to nearly two hours. Although it is the moon that travels and becomes lost to our view, a lunar eclipse looks like a reddish

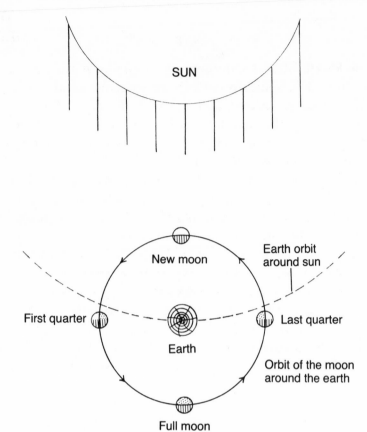

Figure 1.

shadow moving across the bright face of the moon. The reddish glow is caused by light beams being slightly bent by the earth's atmosphere into the shadow of the earth.

A lunar eclipse is visible from any part of the earth from which the moon can be seen. That is why lunar eclipses seem more common, even though they occur only half as often as solar eclipses.

A total solar eclipse takes place only when the moon is new. At this time, the moon is in a position almost directly between the earth and the sun. Although the moon is tiny in comparison to the sun or even to the earth, it is considerably nearer to the earth than it is to the sun. In a direct line-up, the disk of the

20

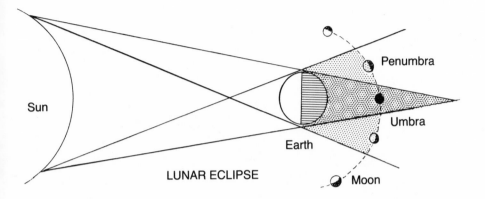

Figure 2.

moon is large enough to hide the more distant disk of the sun. So, as the moon moves slowly into position, the dark circle of the new moon creeps across the face of the sun until the affected part of the earth is left in darkness and the sun seems to disappear (Fig. 3).

Because the shadow cast by the obstructing moon is very narrow, a solar eclipse is visible only within a narrow path traced by the point of the shadow cone as the earth slowly turns (Fig. 4). Even in that narrow path, solar eclipses rarely last more than three to five minutes before the moon moves away from the sun. The moon travels through space at a speed of nearly five thousand miles per hour, when measured in relation to the

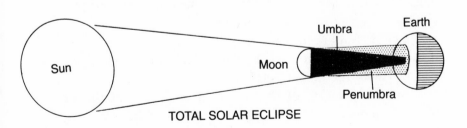

Figure 3.

21

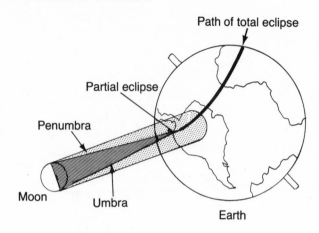

The path traced by a total eclipse is narrow. At the same time, a wider area experiences a partial eclipse.

Figure 4.

movements of the earth. The longest recorded solar eclipse (in June 1955) lasted 7.5 minutes.

Solar and lunar eclipses would occur regularly with every new and full moon *if* the sun, moon, and earth were moving around each other on an even plane, like chess pieces on a tabletop. But that is not the case.

If we picture the earth moving around the sun in an orbit laid out on an imaginary tabletop—a path called the ecliptic— then the path of the moon around the earth is tilted at a slight angle (5°9′), so that part of the orbit passes above and part below the surface of the table top (Fig. 5).

Eclipses can occur only when the new or full moon is in or near the plane of the earth's orbit, which happens only at two points, called the nodes (see N,Fig. 5).

Such a position of the moon in the plane of the earth's orbit happens at *least* twice a year. Both could be solar eclipses, but it is possible to have as many as five solar eclipses and two lunar eclipses visible somewhere on earth within a year's time.

At all other times, the moon passes above or below the plane of the ecliptic, and when that happens, the shadow of the earth is not big enough to reach the moon. Nor can the moon cover the sun enough to cast a shadow on the earth.

Not all solar eclipses are total. Sometimes the deep shadow cone (umbra) of the moon does not reach the surface of the earth. In that case, part of the sun remains visible around the

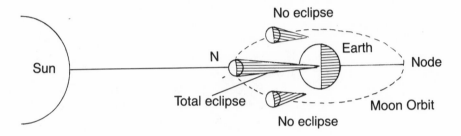

Figure 5.

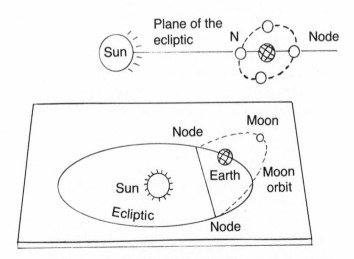

Eclipses can occur only when the paths of the moon and the earth intersect the ecliptic (plane) of the sun at two points called the nodes.

Figure 6.

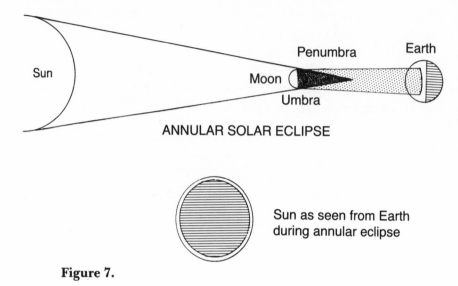

Sun as seen from Earth
during annular eclipse

Figure 7.

dark disk of the moon. This is called an annular eclipse. During an annular eclipse, the earth is partly darkened by a lighter half-shadow called the penumbra (Fig. 7).

There are also partial eclipses when only a small part of the sun is covered by the passing moon. Whenever there is a total eclipse anywhere on earth, neighboring areas experience a partial eclipse.

A partial lunar eclipse occurs whenever the moon enters the earth's penumbra, but usually the effect is so slight that it is barely noticeable.

Like everything else in space, the nodes of the moon are in motion, too. They move from east to west around the earth, reaching the same points in relation to earth once every 18.6 years. But because of the rotation of the earth, even these points are only approximate. The actual interval between two successive solar eclipses in any one spot on earth is about 360 years.

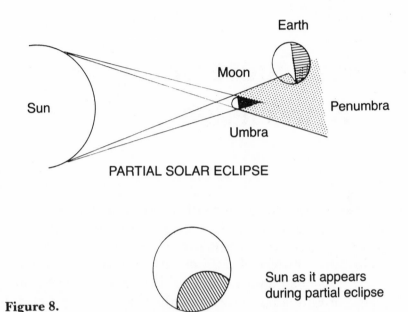

PARTIAL SOLAR ECLIPSE

Figure 8.

Sun as it appears
during partial eclipse

Modern astronomers had to do a tremendous amount of calculating to obtain that figure, taking into account various rates of speed, gravitational pull, and other influences of the moon. In the end, though, what they arrived at was the same old eighteen-year Saros cycle the early Babylonians used to predict eclipses thousands of years ago.

Modern astronomers, however, know *why* the cycles happen—knowledge that eluded the Babylonians and other ancient sky watchers.

The confirmation of the Saros cycles by modern science shows what a fine-tuned mechanism our solar system really is. For over thousands of years, the moving earth, sun, and moon have traveled millions of miles but have intersected each other at the appointed times and places with such precision that clocks can be set by their comings and goings.

Chapter 4

In Quest of Knowledge

In 1915, the great mathematician and physicist Albert Einstein published his famous general theory of relativity, which replaced Newton's theory of gravitation. One part of Einstein's work concerned the way starlight reaches the earth.

People had always assumed that light travels in a straight line. But Einstein proposed that the path of light beams is bent by the gravitational fields of massive bodies of matter. (A gravitational field is the curvature of space around stars and other large solid objects). To test this idea, Einstein suggested that astronomers measure how much starlight is deflected (bent) by the gravitational field of the sun.

To carry out this experiment, one must photograph a group of stars visible at night, fixing their positions in relation to each other. Then the same group of stars must be photographed in daytime, when the sun is between the earth and the group of stars. Of course, the only time these stars can be photographed in daytime is during a total eclipse of the sun. Only then is the sky dark enough for stars to be seen in the daytime.

Astronomers studying the problem selected May 29 (any May 29) as a particularly good time to perform such an experiment, because on that date the sun happens to appear against a particularly large group of stars. By an incredible coincidence, a total eclipse was scheduled to occur on May 29, 1919— only a few years after Einstein's theory was proposed.

A 1724 drawing published with scientific explanations to lessen "the consternation of People Ignorant of ye Causes and Nature of Eclipses of ye Sun and Moon."

Several teams of astronomers prepared to use that eclipse to test the new theory. Different teams in different parts of the world were to photograph the same star field at night and during the eclipse.

The experiment worked. The stars photographed at night were clearly in different positions when compared with the same group photographed during the eclipse. This proved that the presence of the sun between earth and the stars has an effect on the path of the light beams. (Since 1919, the same experiment has been carried out during a number of solar eclipses, always with the same result.) Proving Einstein's theory is one dramatic way eclipses have been used to advance scientific knowledge over the centuries.

Astronomy is, of course, the most obvious discipline to benefit from eclipse research. The earliest sky watchers learned during eclipses that stars are present even in the daytime sky, although they are invisible because of the bright glow of the sun. This may be obvious to us, but to people who thought of the stars, the sun, and the moon as great lights set out by the gods to brighten the night, it must have been a surprising revelation.

Figure 9. Total eclipse of the sun: the corona and prominences become visible. (drawn from a photograph)

In more recent times, astronomers have used eclipses to learn new facts about the sun and the moon. Ordinarily, all we can see of the sun with the naked eye, or even with small telescopes, is the luminous solar disc or photosphere (ball of light). But the main body of the sun, like the earth, is surrounded by a layer of gases called the atmosphere, the upper thin layer or shell of which is called the corona. The corona reaches about a million miles into space from the surface of the sun. But because its glow is not as bright as that of the sun itself, it is normally invisible. During solar eclipses, when the moon blots out the bright glow of the sun itself, the corona suddenly appears in all its splendor.

Astrophysicists have learned many things about the sun's size, temperature, and chemical composition by studying the corona during different eclipses. Eclipse research has revealed the turbulent nature of the gaseous layer just above the edge (limb) of the solar disk. This layer is called the chromosphere (meaning "ball of color"). Tall, luminous clouds of gas, called prominences, thrust upward into the corona. Some produce spectacular eruptions, which throw out tall bursts of flaming material far from the edge of the sun. Even larger flaming masses called helmet streamers may stretch above the chromosphere into the lower corona. And tall solar flares called polar plumes sometimes soar upward from the sun's polar regions.

All these observations help scientists learn more about the nature of the sun. They have also taught astronomers something about the surface of the moon. During total eclipses, just before the disk of the moon covers the disk of the sun, a narrow, ragged edge of light around the moon remains visible. In time astronomers realized that this raggedness is formed by some rather formidable mountains at the edge of the moon. The effect is called Baily's Beads, named after the astronomer Francis Baily, who first recorded those features in 1836.

For many years, much effort was devoted during eclipses to locating a possible tenth planet in our solar system. Urbaine Jean Joseph Leverrier, a French astronomer, speculated in 1845 that such a new planet existed near the orbit of Mercury. He named it Vulcan, after the Roman god of fire. The idea of such an unknown planet stirred the imagination of sky watchers everywhere.

But new knowledge about the inner solar system provided by today's space program has made it quite evident that such an extra planet does not exist in that location. Nevertheless people persist in spotting unknown "objects" near the sun during eclipses. As recently as 1966, and again in 1970, such an object was reported by Professor Henry Courten of Dowling College on Long Island, New York. Professor Courten did not claim that the object was the mythical planet Vulcan, but his reports revived speculation.

Astronomers still haven't ruled out the possibility that another planet might exist somewhere in the outer portions of our solar system. As the explorer spacecraft Pioneer 10 moves

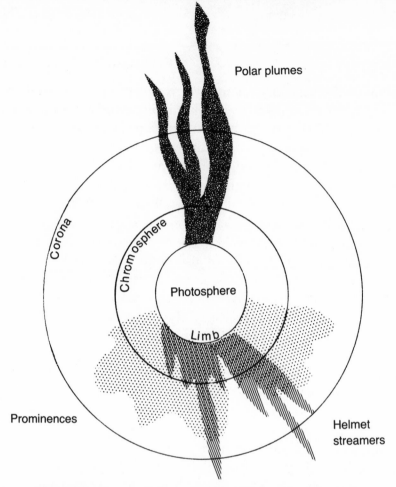

Figure 10. Solar activities visible briefly when the very bright photosphere is covered by the moon's shadow during an eclipse.

away from the sun toward interstellar space, some scientists hope it might encounter the source of a strange gravitational pull near Uranus and Neptune—a source that could turn out to be an unseen Planet X.

Another somewhat elusive research project carried out during eclipses involves a strange light pattern known as shadow bands. Many people have reported seeing these colorful bands of light moving across the landscape just ahead of the shadow of an eclipse. The patterns are particularly evident against such neutral backgrounds as sand dunes or a desert.

Corona: *The atmosphere of the sun (yellow/green).*
Chromosphere *("ball of color"): Brilliant red layer of gases (mostly hydrogen and calcium).*
Photosphere *("ball of light"): The visible disk of the sun.*
Limb: *The edge of the solar disk.*
Prominences: *Luminous clouds of gas within the corona.*
Helmet Streamers: *Shooting flares surging across the prominences in the lower corona.*
Polar Plumes: *Tall flares spewing upward from the polar regions of the sun through the corona and beyond.*
Nucleus: *Frozen center of gravel, dust, and ice.*
Coma: *Halo of gases.*
Head: *The combined nucleus and coma.*
Tail: *Long trail of gases swept backward from the coma when the comet nears the sun (the tail always points away from the sun).*

Some people believe that the bands are caused by the refraction (deflection) of the narrow slit of sunlight shining through layers of atmosphere with different densities. Others believe that they are caused by sunlight being deflected by the edge of the moon. No one really has the answer. And not all eclipse watchers manage to see the shadow-band effect. Nevertheless, shadow-band research continues during eclipses.

Astronomers are not the only scientists gathering information during eclipses. Early geographers and surveyors found eclipse data useful to determine the measurements of longitudes. By observing the exact location of a projected eclipse, geographers could chart that location on a map. The early Greeks used lunar eclipses for this purpose. By observing the local times at which lunar eclipses were seen in two different places and then calculating the difference, they were able to pinpoint the difference in longitudes.

Historians and archaeologists have been using eclipse data to verify historical records for a long time. Since dates in ancient records are often identified only by the reigns of kings or wars, historians have searched for reports about eclipses taking place during specific wars or reigns, since even past eclipses can be dated with clockwork precision.

Eclipse information has also been useful in calculating the rate of movement of the earth, sun, and moon. In 1695 the famous astronomer Edmund Halley compared ancient eclipse records with current observations of the movements of the moon to show that the moon had increased its rate of speed over the centuries. In more recent times, astronomers have sought to prove through solar eclipse data that the earth's rate of rotation is slowing down.

In 1675, the Danish astronomer Ole Romer used eclipse data based on eclipses of the moons of Jupiter to prove that light takes time to travel, and he measured the rate of speed. Experiments involving optics, photography, and photometry are still carried out during eclipses today. Other scientists perform experiments involving radio waves, meteorology, and atmospheric pressures. Biologists, too, can profit from eclipse research. Animal behavior during eclipses has been studied and observed for years. Even untrained observers have noted that birds will tuck their heads under their wings—as if settling down to sleep—when the shadow of an eclipse darkens the earth. Sheep and cattle will lie down. Bees will return to their hives.

Ocean creatures also react to the changes in light during eclipses. Even the microscopic colonies of sea life, such as plankton, respond to the darkening of the sky during eclipses by rising toward the surface of the ocean just as they do at night.

Finally, eclipses provide an opportunity for scientists to probe the skies for such occasional space wanderers as comets, asteroids, and "shooting stars," even though such studies are carried out more efficiently today by space probes and orbiting man-made satellites.

Chapter 5

The Eclipse Hunters

"Observations of eclipses have been attended with so many advantages to mankind that they are universally esteemed objects of Great Attention in every civilized nation."

These words are part of a petition that was presented to the Council of the House of Representatives in 1780 by Reverend Samuel Williams, a professor of mathematics and natural philosophy at Harvard University. The petition requested help from the legislature to permit a group of Harvard scientists to travel to Penobscot Bay (in what is now the state of Maine) in order to view the total solar eclipse scheduled to be visible from that location on October 27, 1780.

Why did scientists have to enlist the help of the government for a scientific expedition? The problem was a matter of war. In 1780 the young American republic was still fighting the Revolutionary War, and, inconveniently, Penobscot Bay had recently been retaken by the British. The site of the projected scientific expedition lay in enemy territory.

What to do? Reverend Williams decided to ask the British for safe-conduct for his expedition, pointing out the importance of his scientific task. After all, eclipses were rare events that would not wait for the end of a war. There wouldn't be another opportunity to see an eclipse in the general area for another twenty-six years.

Harvard University, the American Academy of Arts and Sciences, and the Massachusetts legislature all supported Williams in his request. John Hancock, the speaker of the House, pleaded with the British commander at Penobscot Bay to make the American expedition possible.

Addressing the commander as a "Friend of Science," Hancock wrote: "Though we are political enemies, yet with regard to Science it is presumable we shall not dissent from the practice of all civilized people in promoting it either in conjunction or separately as occasions for it shall happen to offer."

Apparently the British, too, recognized the importance of the mission. They granted the expedition safe-conduct. And so, on October 9, 1780, Reverend Williams set out from Boston in the sloop *Lincoln*, accompanied by three colleagues and six students.

Their main purpose was to gather necessary information for more accurate longitude measurements. They carried with them boxes of instruments and the latest map of the area, published in 1776, which showed in great detail Penobscot Bay and the land around it. The heavy weight of their scientific equipment was actually the reason they had to set up camp in enemy territory. The western portion of Penobscot Bay was the only place in the path of the eclipse accessible by a ship large enough to carry the equipment.

All went well, including the weather. The eclipse arrived on schedule, and Reverend Williams described what he could see: "The sun's limb became so small as to appear like a circular thread, or rather like a very fine horn. Both the ends lost their acuteness, and seemed to break off in the form of small drops or stars. . . ."

Williams waited with great excitement for the moment of totality. It never came. The eclipse had started at 12:28:48. By 12:31:18 he was forced to admit that "it was evident that the broken parts of the sun's limb began to increase and unite." Moreover, others noted that brightness was beginning to increase.

Something had gone wrong. Months of calculating and surveying had been wasted. The place the expedition had chosen to watch the eclipse had been outside the path of totality. For Reverend Williams, it was a bitter disappointment. While his observations provided accurate comparisons for longitude calculations, his choice of the wrong spot disturbed him greatly. He wondered about the accuracy of his instruments. He blamed his maps.

In 1980 a group of Harvard students and professors traveled to Maine to reenact Williams's experiment. They used the same instruments used by the original expedition and carried with them some of the same maps that may have been used in 1780. They found that the instruments performed flawlessly and that the maps were amazingly accurate. Williams had erred in his calculations of latitude. He had set up his instruments thirty miles farther south than astronomical tables indicated he should. It was a simple error. The expedition that had managed to make a war step aside for the sake of science missed witnessing totality because of a mathematical miscalculation.

The Williams expedition was the first American attempt to study a total solar eclipse, but European scientists had tried to chase after eclipses ever since the true nature and the scientific importance of these events was first understood. It wasn't an easy task. Often the best places to observe total eclipses are in the middle of an ocean, in mountainous areas, remote deserts, or other inaccessible spots. Before the middle of the nineteenth century, traveling to these faraway places required enormous expense and stamina, if they could be reached at all. Then there was always the weather. Scientists might travel great distances with heavy loads of equipment only to find that clouds covered the sky above their chosen observation points, so all their efforts were in vain. In view of these difficulties, it is amazing how many eclipses were studied by early scientific observers and how much information was gathered.

The invention of photography in 1839 added a new dimension to the recording of eclipses and was first used to capture an eclipse in 1851. Now scientists had to cope with even more instruments requiring careful handling and transportation. But photography made the spectacular effects of solar eclipses visible to many ordinary people. It was one thing to see an artist's representation of an eclipse in a newspaper or magazine engraving. But it was a much more immediate experience to see the step-by-step progression of the eclipse captured in a series of photographs. It made people want to see these spectacular sky shows for themselves.

But eclipse-chasing remained difficult and expensive. It required costly and cumbersome expeditions planned years before the scheduled event. Only dedicated scientists were included in such expeditions. Other people rarely got to see an eclipse unless its path happened to pass right through the area where they lived.

And yet the most vivid and poetic descriptions of eclipses come from people who have watched them for sheer pleasure, rather than for scientific enrichment.

One such eyewitness was Mabel Loomis Todd, the wife of one astronomer and the daughter of another. She accompanied her husband on several expeditions organized by Amherst College, in Massachusetts, where Professor Todd taught. She recorded her eclipse-chasing experiences in a series of travel books.

One trip in 1896 took her to northern Japan. On another occasion, in 1900, she accompanied an expedition to the Barbary Coast in North Africa. For both trips, a large yacht was used to transport the scientists and their equipment.

As the only member of the party free from specific tasks, Mrs. Todd had plenty of opportunity to observe everything that was happening around her as the shadow of the moon slowly moved across the face of the sun.

In Japan the expedition was set up overlooking a river mouth. Mrs. Todd described the dramatic beginning of the eclipse when, as it grew darker, "sampans and junks faded together into colorlessness; but grass and verdure turned suddenly vivid yellow green. A penetrating chill fell over the land."

As the moon gradually advanced, "the visible world seemed drifting into the deathly trance which eclipses always produce. . . . I saw the strange wavering light and darkness. . . . I thought of drifting smoke. . . . I was seeing actual 'shadow bands'—that strange quiver of mystery which creeps or rushes or glides across the world just before the moon's shadow completely envelops the landscape." Mrs. Todd also noticed that the many gulls that had swooped across the river suddenly disappeared.

"Then instantaneous darkness leaped upon the world. Unearthly night enveloped all." The next instant, "with an indescribable out-flashing . . . the corona burst forth in mysterious radiance. But dimly seen through thin cloud, it was nevertheless beautiful beyond description, a celestial flame from some unimaginable heaven."

All at once the sky was flooded with a lurid and brilliant orange, with darker clouds moving "like liquid flame, or huge ejecta from some vast volcanic Hades. . . . Absolute silence reigned. No bird twittered. Even the sighing of the surf breathed into utter repose, and not a ripple stirred the leaden sea."

To Mrs. Todd, it was an awe-inspiring moment: "It was as if the hand of Deity had been visibly laid upon space and worlds, to allow one momentary glimpse of the awfulness of Creation."

The glimpse was brief. Totality lasted only two and a half minutes. Mrs. Todd noted, perhaps with regret, "When the tiniest globule of sunlight, a drop, a needle-shaft, a pin-hole reappeared . . . the fair corona and all color in sky and cloud withdrew, and a natural aspect of stormy twilight returned."

Mrs. Todd was equally poetic when she described the 1900 eclipse from a rooftop in Tripoli. Writing about the beginning of that event, she remarked that "the first 'bite' into his dazzling disk had been taken, and silently on-creeping, the sun's extinguisher covered more and more of the shining surface until only a stout crescent remained."

She noted that the color of everything visible was "sad, subdued; the sapphire sea became a cold slate, the sky like steel. . . . It became cool and damp, and the swallows emerged in flocks, flying about excitedly in a manner quite unlike their nightly sunset parade. Camels dropped upon their knees, and other animals exhibited much uneasiness."

Moments later, "totality was upon us. It came . . . in a silent unfolding, inexpressibly majestic and lovely. One second the luminous drops, as the shining crescent broke up—the next, there hung the great black ball of the moon in the clear gray-purple sky, while around it blossomed the exquisite corona, like some fair flower of celestial light. . . . This corona glowed in elusive fairy-like beauty, while planets emerged in the cool sky, and a hush as of eternal waiting pervaded the still air."

And it took only fifty seconds to experience all of that!

Mabel Loomis Todd probably acquired her enthusiasm from her father, who had spent much of his life chasing after eclipses. He described one expedition undertaken in 1889 for the U.S. government on the U.S.S. navy ship *Pensacola*, on which his future son-in-law, David P. Todd, was the chief of expedition. The journey took the party to Angola, in West Africa.

This was an adventurous undertaking in that era. Professor Loomis wrote about visits from cannibals to their camp on Cape Ledo, and about his worries over the safety of the equipment in view of prowling animals and native intruders. Wisely, the members of the expedition had waited out the days until the actual eclipse on board the ship, which was anchored just offshore. A moment of panic came when a strange green light was glimpsed over the beach. The scientists had rigged up a set of red and green lights to warn them of intruders near their equipment. It turned out to be a strangely appropriate false alarm. What the ship's party had witnessed was the passage of a bright green meteor streaking across the black sky the night before the eclipse.

Mr. Loomis kept notes during the eclipse, minute by minute. At 1:35 A.M., a rift in the clouds showed a partial eclipse.

At 2:35, "over the sea rushed this blue-black shadow of the moon. . . . It seemed like the approach of a storm, though the air was still. Then a pale yellow light, like dawn, swept in . . . and all was normal."

At 2:48, the light assumed an unusual appearance, ominous and threatening. Half a minute later came the first slight dimming of light: "The white sails of a vessel vanished, flocks of carrion crows hurried from seaward as if bewildered, seeking a place to perch. Wydah birds ceased their cries."

Dark shadows, bright yellow light, a strange hush in the air. . . . The experiences of eclipse watchers always seem to be amazingly similar. Wherever and whenever people have watched total solar eclipses, they have come away with a sense of reverence and awe. No wonder those who had the money, stamina, and sense of adventure braved hardships to see for themselves.

A modern poet, Annie Dillard, reacted similarly to an eclipse she watched from a hilltop near Tacoma, Washington, on February 26, 1979: "It began with no ado," she wrote in her book *Teaching a Stone to Talk*. "Without pause or preamble, silent as orbits, a piece of the sun went away. . . . A piece of the sun was missing; in its place we saw empty sky. . . . The sun was going and the world was wrong. The grasses were wrong; they were platinum. . . . The hillside was a nineteenth-century tinted photograph from which the tint had faded. . . . The sky was a navy blue. My hands were silver."

Afterward she remembered that "a wall of shadow came speeding towards the assembled watchers and they screamed before it hit."

Annie Dillard did not think what she saw looked like the moon. If she had not known it was the moon, it would never have occurred to her. But she could understand why people might have thought of dragons in the past, or why some people were said to have died of fright when experiencing an eclipse.

Eclipse-hunting remained a "sport" reserved for serious scientists until well past the middle of our own century. But in

1963 a young eclipse enthusiast dreamed up a plan that would bring the eclipse-watching experience to a lot of other enthusiastic and curious people.

Marcy Pedas, a Greek-American college girl from a small steel town in Pennsylvania, had come to Trois Rivières in Canada with her astronomer brother and a friend to watch the eclipse of July 20, 1963. It was an unforgettable experience.

As Marcy watched the sky turn colors and darken, and the sun seem to disappear, she felt herself reacting the way her Greek shepherd ancestors might have reacted on a similar occasion. As the seconds and minutes of darkness ticked by, something within Marcy strongly wanted the darkness to go away and the sun to reappear. And yet, when it was over and the sun had broken free from the moon's dark shadow, Marcy knew that this was something she wanted to experience again. Having been thrilled by what she had seen, she wanted to share the experience with others.

As it turned out, the next eclipse she could hope to attend would cross the northeastern United States on March 7, 1970. Seven years is a long time to wait. Marcy finished college, married the friend who had watched the Canadian eclipse with her, and went to work as an elementary-school teacher. But her dreams about organizing an eclipse party for a group of interested friends stayed in her mind. She studied the maps. The 1970 eclipse would be visible from many places along the East Coast. To Marcy's delight, one place in its path was a tiny town near Norfolk, Virginia, called Eclipse.

What a suitable place for an eclipse party, she thought. And so, early in 1970, she traveled to Eclipse to see if she could book hotel or motel reservations for a sizable group.

To Marcy's dismay, the people of Eclipse wanted no part of such a project. Fearful of what a large group of outsiders might do, the townspeople of Eclipse refused to cooperate. Defeated, Marcy, along with her husband, Phil, and her brother, Ted, left Virginia to look for another suitable site. They explored the island of Nantucket, off the coast of Massachusetts, that was to be in the path of the eclipse. But Nantucket, even with all its hotels and guest houses, showed no interest in housing a group of amateur astronomers. Traveling back to Cape Cod on the ferry, Marcy sadly went over the list of requirements for staging an eclipse party. She needed a place large enough to assemble a sizable crowd and equipped with bathrooms and restaurant facilities.

There ought to be places like that, she thought. Even the ferry had most of these requirements—bathrooms, food, space to set up telescopes and other instruments.

The ferry! It was a crazy idea, but it might work. Why not watch the eclipse from the deck of a ship? A ship could be steered to the best possible vantage point.

As it turned out, ferries may operate only within their own established runs. But the idea of an eclipse party on board a ship had been born. It was too late to organize such a cruise for the 1970 eclipse, but another one was practically around the corner in 1972. With renewed enthusiasm, Marcy set out to find a ship whose crew was willing to sail to Nova Scotia in June 1972.

It was a difficult search. Most shipping companies laughed at the request from a penniless young woman without experience in the travel field to charter a ship for a cruise to an offbeat part of the Atlantic Ocean. By now Marcy and Phil had enlarged their dream to include many more people than their own group of personal friends. They were sure they would find enough astronomy buffs to fill a ship if they advertised in astronomy magazines. Finally, a small Greek shipping line agreed to provide a ship if Marcy could produce a sufficient number of paying customers by a certain date. With misgivings, Marcy and Phil dug into their meager savings to pay for the ads in the astronomy magazines and planetarium newsletters.

To their amazement, and to that of the shipping line, reservations with deposit checks began to pour in. Before long, the line had booked more passengers for the eclipse cruise than for any of the regular cruises. Still there were obstacles. The most serious one occurred when the captain declared that, according to shipping regulations, he would have to turn on the ship's lights when the sky grew dark during the eclipse. That, of course, would prevent a clear view of the eclipse and would make photography difficult. Angrily, Marcy sat down and addressed letters to some six hundred paid-up customers to an-

The camera captured two moments of the solar eclipse of 1973: The first, taken just seconds before totality, shows the so-called diamond-ring effect; the second records totality. Note that the corona is clearly visible when the solar disk is obscured.

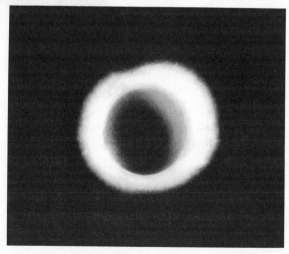

nounce that the trip would have to be canceled. With the box of stamped and addressed letters under her arm, she stormed into the offices of the shipping company and announced her ultimatum: Either the captain would agree to keep the lights off during the eclipse, or the cancellation letters would go directly into the nearest mailbox.

Marcy won. On June 8, 1972, her first eclipse cruise, with 830 passengers on board, sailed from New York to the waters off Nova Scotia. Two days later, at 3:47 P.M., the travelers observed a total eclipse under nearly perfect weather conditions. Crowded on the decks, the eclipse-hunters observed the approaching black shadow of the moon—a black shape something like a tornado—and the "diamond ring" effect, which showed up just before the moon fully covered the face of the sun. They watched the bright coronal streamers protruding from the edge of the sun. Some noted the slight drop in temperature, the eerie light that cast a ghostlike pallor over people and objects alike. And they spoke about changes in the color of the sea, which began to turn a deep purple as the eclipse proceeded toward totality.

The amateur eclipse-hunters had been carefully briefed on how to observe and photograph an eclipse safely without damaging their eyes. Precautions included the use of pinhole cameras and special smoked glasses to protect their eyes from the burning rays of the sun. It is never safe to watch an eclipse without these protective devices until after totality is reached. (See Appendix 3.)

The 1972 expedition was such a success that many more have taken place since then. While later eclipse cruises attracted many scientists, science writers, astronauts, and astronomers, the bulk of the passenger list was still made up of ordinary people—schoolteachers, students, and photography buffs. Marcy's dream of sharing her excitement with others was fulfilled, and she created a special occupation for herself—a Pied Piper of sorts for those who share her own special sense of curiosity, adventure, and wonder.

Chapter 6

Flaming Swords
and Crystal Tresses

When we look up at a clear, cloudless night sky, the pattern of visible stars is usually reassuringly familiar. Although the movements of stars, planets, and the earth cause these patterns to "travel" nightly and seasonally through the sky, the changes are small, slow, and predictable—*so* predictable, in fact, that travelers on land and sea for thousands of years have used the stars as directional signposts. Occasionally, though, there are interlopers among the familiar figures. Brighter, larger, and faster than ordinary stars, these "space invaders" move through and among such familiar constellations as the Big Dipper and the Seven Sisters, dragging behind them long trails of light.

To the people in the ancient world, these strange "shooting stars" were even more frightening than eclipses. For one thing, there were more of them. Several might appear in any one year, arriving mysteriously one night, growing larger and brighter month by month, and finally disappearing just as mysteriously. To people who gave godlike qualities to all heavenly bodies, these periodic space travelers were thought to be special messengers bringing bad news.

Our universe is a busy place. All kinds of rocky and gaseous bodies move among the stars and planets, tracing their own special orbits through space. One special group are known as comets, a name derived from the Greek word komētēs, meaning "long-haired." They were given that name because many people thought they looked like strange beings with large heads trailing long manes of hair.

A comet is, in fact, a large ball of ice and dust enveloped in a huge cloud of gas. In its orbit around the sun, the gaseous cloud occasionally streams behind the head of the comet like a long, shimmering tail. Modern astronomers can study the shape of comets through telescopes, watching them arrive in our solar system long before they are visible to the naked eye and observing the way they change as the heat of our sun causes some of the frozen particles to release those flaming tails of gas.

Our earliest ancestors, however, did not understand that these moving lights were nothing but huge masses of gas, dirt, and ice. They watched these strange bright stars bear down toward them, coming closer and closer each night, and they saw in them threatening shapes and creatures that seemed to foreshadow evil.

There are many descriptions of comets in ancient literature. In the Bible, for instance, we find this passage in the Book of Revelation: "There appeared another wonder in Heaven; and behold a great red dragon. . . . and his tail drew the third part of the stars of Heaven. . . ."

St. John did not identify this vision specifically as a comet, but it fits the image of comets as described by other writers. A report about the comet of December 14, 1000, also mentions a dragon—a blue-footed one with a growing head.

Other writers described comets as flaming swords, as curved arms holding swords, or as disks, casks, spears, or torches. Some saw bearded faces with bristling hair or horse heads with blood-colored manes. There were so many different descriptions that the first-century Roman naturalist Pliny finally classified comets by their shape, length, and brilliance of tails, and divided them into twelve different categories. Pliny also saw in some comets the image of God in human form because of their intense whiteness.

While everybody seemed to see something else when they looked at a passing comet, most people agreed that comets were celestial messengers sent to foretell good and bad events— mostly bad, according to the poets, historians, and philosophers.

An old German rhyme sums it up:

Eight things there be a comet brings. . . .
Wind, Famine, Plague, Death to Kings,
War, Earthquakes, Floods, and Direful Change.

In the *Iliad*, which was written during the ninth century B.C., the Greek poet Homer spoke just as harshly about comets:

Like the red star, that from his flaming hair
Shakes down diseases, pestilence and war

Centuries later, the English poet John Milton used the same imagery in *Paradise Lost* when he described a comet that "from its horrid hair shakes pestilence and war."

There were some who regarded comets a little more kindly. The ancient Romans believed that comets were the souls of illustrious people being carried to heaven. Others felt that the bright lights of comets were simply signs that some notable person had died.

In his play *Julius Caesar*, William Shakespeare wrote:

When beggars die, there are no comets seen
The Heavens themselves blaze forth the death of Princes.

And in *Henry IV*, he saw a comet almost as an avenger, rather than the cause of a king's death:

Comets importing change of time and states
Brandish your crystal tresses to the sky
And with them scourge the bad revolting stars
That have consented unto Henry's death.

Because of the widespread fear of comets, their appearance must have provided steady employment for soothsayers

An eighteenth-century engraving showing the bright path of a comet above a Swiss monastery.

and magicians. After a while, comet predictions became a science of sorts. Sword-shaped comets, for example, were said to foreshadow war. A "hairy" comet, on the other hand, was an omen that a king would die.

In fact, the appearance of comets did precede the deaths of Julius Caesar, the emperor Nero, King Merovingus, Pope Urban IV, the prophet Mahomet, and Attila the Hun, among others. In 79 A.D., when the Roman emperor Vespasian was told about a newly sighted "hairy" comet, he was in the middle of a war and refused to be frightened. The comet could not possibly foretell his death, he claimed, since he was totally bald. It had to be a sign that his well-tressed opponent would come to grief. But Vespasian did die shortly after the comet sighting, thus reinforcing the ancient superstition.

These beliefs were so strong that occasionally the appearance of a comet actually drove a king to his death. King Louis the Debonair of France, the son of Charlemagne, accepted the

During the Middle Ages, people imagined that they could see menacing bloodied swords and bearded faces when they looked at a comet passing through the sky.

comet of 837 as a sign that he would die. And, in a frenzied attempt to stave off the inevitable, he gave donations to monasteries, built churches, ordered the saying of masses, and gave himself over to prayer. It did not help. He died in 840. Those he left behind were sure he died of fear.

Another emperor, Charles V of Germany and Spain, was said to have given up his crown and become a monk in response to the appearance of the comet of 1556—perhaps in an attempt to save his life. It is a good story, but one made up long after the fact, because in truth, Charles gave up his crown in 1555, and the comet did not appear until a year later.

According to another story, the famous general Hannibal committed suicide in 183 B.C. because of the appearance of a comet. It is more likely, though, that Hannibal was despondent because he had lost a war against the Romans and did not want to surrender.

A sixteenth-century drawing that includes the swords and bearded, severed heads so often "seen" in comets during the Middle Ages.

There are a great many stories told to "document" the effect of sword-shaped comets on battles, wars, and other conflicts. Some have linked sword-shaped comets to the flaming swords which barred a sinful Adam and Eve from the Garden of Eden in the Old Testament. In others, a comet heralded Noah's great deluge. More historically correct is a report by the Hebrew historian Josephus, who wrote about the great flaming sword hanging in the night skies over besieged Jerusalem for weeks before the fall of that great city in 70 A.D. Josephus complained that the Jews refused to heed the comet's warning.

The loss of Constantinople in 1453 was blamed on a comet, as was the outbreak of the Thirty Years' War in 1618 and the defeat of Napoleon in Russia in 1811. William the Conqueror felt that a three-tailed comet in 1066 gave him the right to invade England because the omen meant that England needed a new king.

To some people, certain comets were seen as *good* omens. In 1456 a great comet appeared over eastern Europe while Pope Calixtus III was at war with the Saracens in Belgrade. This same comet was also seen over China, where it was described as having a tail sixty feet long "like a peacock's, with a head the size of a bull's eye." To Pope Calixtus, however, the comet seemed to be shaped like a cross, while to his Muslim opponent, it was shaped like a scimitar. Both rulers blessed the comet and claimed its powers for their own side.

The Christians won this particular encounter—a victory still celebrated in Italy during the Festival of the Transfiguration. On that day, certain cakes called *cometes* are sold at the church doors. Some people think that these cakes were named in honor of that fateful comet.

There are stories about other cross-shaped comets. Constantine the Great, the first Christian emperor of Rome, supposedly converted to Christianity when he saw such a comet in the midst of a battle. Here, too, the comet was seen as beneficial. There are also tales connecting the appearances of comets with the births of such great religious leaders as Krishna, Buddha, Lao Tsu, Aesculapius, Abraham, and Moses. And the Star of Bethlehem, which heralded the birth of Jesus, might well have been one of the frequent appearances of the flaming ball of dirt and gas that we now know as Halley's Comet.

In spite of these exceptions, however, comets generally have received bad press. They have been blamed not only for wars and massacres, but for floods, famines, pestilences, and epidemics as well. The busy astrologers and soothsayers who interpreted their meanings could not be doubted, for if a predicted event did not happen, they could always claim that they had averted the disaster through skillful use of magic or prayer. To load the dice even more, the "rules" said that a predicted event could be postponed for as many years as the number of *days* the comet had remained visible! So it wasn't difficult to find some disaster or conflict to blame on the temporary visitor in the skies. In England, the Great Plague of 1664 and the Great Fire of London in 1666 were both blamed on comets that had appeared years earlier. It was said that the one warning of the plague was pale, while the one that came before the fire sparkled.

All these superstitions about comets lingered long into more rational ages. The earliest New World colonists even brought them along. One Puritan minister, Increase Mather, preached of the dire warnings brought by comets. And as late as 1910, during the appearance of a comet, sheriffs in Oklahoma "arrived just in time to prevent the sacrifice of a virgin by demented Americans calling themselves 'Select Followers,'" according to a 1981 book by Nigel Calder.

People fear what they do not understand. And until quite recently, people really did not understand the nature of comets. No wonder they listened to the persuasive words of their poets—the eighteenth-century poet James Thomson, for example, who wrote:

> *Lo! From the dread insecurity of space*
> *Returning with accelerated course,*
> *The rushing Comet to the sun descends:*
> *And as he shrinks below the shading earth*
> *With awful train projected o'er the heavens*
> *The guilty nations tremble.*

Or, even more convincingly, from this unknown poet:

> *The blazing star*
> *Threatening the world with famine, plague and war*
> *To princes death, to kingdoms many curses*
> *To all estates inevitable losses*
> *To herdsmen rot; to ploughmen hapless seasons*
> *To sailors storms; to cities civil treason.*

Chapter 7

Comet Facts
and Comet Fiction

In May 1773, the people of Paris sat in their homes waiting for the world to come to an end. The cause of their fears was a comet that was approaching rapidly on a seemingly straight course toward collision with the earth. The date of projected impact was May 20, 1773, and the scientists of the day predicted that this collision would pulverize the earth. For days, many Parisians prayed or spent their money recklessly in preparation for the end. Some unscrupulous skeptics even sold places in heaven, it is said, to those who were not quite sure of their final destination—making a quick profit out of piety and fear.

Needless to say, the world was not crushed by the Comet of 1773, which passed harmlessly on its way through our solar system.

In 1832 there was another scare. The Comet Biela was on a path destined to cross the orbit of the earth on October 29. Once again there were predictions of collisions and destruction. In fact, the earth did not reach that particular spot on its orbital path until November 30. The comet had passed harmlessly more than a month earlier.

In 1861 the earth passed safely through the tail of a large comet. Nevertheless, less than fifty years later, in 1910, the approach of another comet triggered dire warnings that "poisoned air" would be brought to Earth in the comet's tail. It was

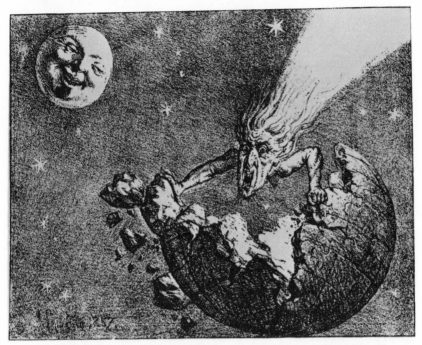

During a comet scare in 1857, a French artist imagined the disaster that might befall if the comet should strike Earth, as predicted, on June 13 that year. The fears proved unfounded.

believed that when combined with the nitrogen of our atmosphere, the gases of the tail would produce a chemical substance similar to the laughing gas then widely used in dentists' offices. To cash in on this fear, some people sold "comet pills" to safeguard against laughing-gas poisoning. Others believed that if they were mixed with the hydrogen in the atmosphere, comet gases might cause horrendous explosions on the earth.

These stories are examples of what might be called "scientific superstitions." Long after people had stopped believing in flaming swords and hairy monsters as harbingers of death and war, comet lore continued to be full of misconceptions and strange ideas. Some of these ideas *sounded* scientific. For example, one theory held that comets affected the brain, producing violent impulses in the people living below their orbits. Other theories held that comets affected the spring tides or brought flu epidemics in their wake. Still others held that comets might fall into the sun and thus produce greater heat, which, in turn, might destroy our planet.

The very nature of comets was not understood until recent times. They were variously described as reflections of the sun, colored air, sparks from an elemental fire, or starlight seen through a cloud. Some thought they were the coming together of several stars, which produced a very bright light in the sky. Others spoke of "dry and inflamed exhalations"; "fiery terrestrial matter caught in the wind"; and "elevated clouds." Certain early Chaldeans and Greeks came closer to scientific accuracy when they spoke of comets as planets or groups of planets.

If all these ideas are false, what then is true?

In simple terms, a comet is a loose collection of ice, rocks, and gravel, surrounded by a cloudlike mass of very fine dust and gases that is sometimes blown backward to form a burning "tail." The appearance of a comet depends somewhat upon its distance from the sun. Far from the sun, it is mostly a ball of ice and dust. But as the frozen gases are warmed by the sun, the mixture becomes gaseous again, thus forming the cloudlike halo. The solid center of the comet is called the *nucleus*. The surrounding halo of gases is called the *coma*, from the Latin word for hair—another reference to those hairy monsters seen in ancient times. The nucleus and the coma together form the head of the comet, compared to its trailing tail. The nucleus may be round or oval—or even tubular—and there can be more than one. Some comets also have more than one tail. The Comet of 1744 was described as having six tails.

Comets come in many sizes. The nucleus can be as small as thirty miles across and as large as eight thousand miles. The size of comet heads ranges from eighteen thousand miles in diameter to well over one million miles. Tails range in length from nineteen million miles to more than two hundred million. Some comets are larger than the orbit of the moon around the earth, and many of them appear to be as large as the moon when they reach their closest distance from the earth.

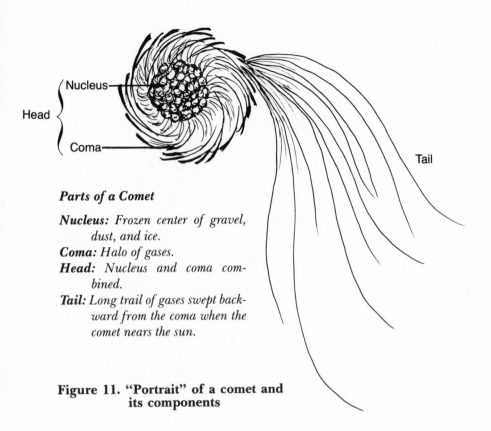

Nucleus

Head

Coma

Tail

Parts of a Comet

Nucleus: *Frozen center of gravel, dust, and ice.*
Coma: *Halo of gases.*
Head: *Nucleus and coma combined.*
Tail: *Long trail of gases swept backward from the coma when the comet nears the sun.*

Figure 11. "Portrait" of a comet and its components

The color of comets varies, too, from silvery gray to yellow to ruddy red. Some have appeared in a night sky shining as brightly as the sun. Yet comets are insubstantial. They can pass in front of a star without dimming its light.

This is how the Greek poet Virgil, who lived in the first century B.C., described a comet in *The Aeneid*: "Scarce had the old man ceased from praying when a peal of thunder was heard on the left, and a star, gliding from the heavens amid the darkness, rushed through space followed by a long train of light."

It is simple to describe a comet, but it is harder to figure out how one originated. There are about three hundred billion comets floating around in our solar system (which is only a very small corner of our vast universe). Some astronomers believe that comets may be mini–solar systems, circling a rocky core

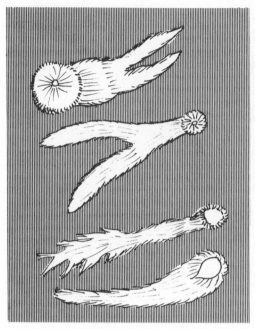
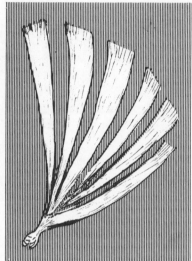

The six-tailed Comet of 1744

Different views of one comet as seen at different times

Figure 12. The varied shapes of comets

produced by the explosion of a planet that once may have existed between Mars and Jupiter. Others say comets are simply leftover space debris, formed when our solar system was formed, but not included within any of the larger planets, moons, and other satellites. They may have been formed in the outer region of the original nebular disk from which our solar system sprang. And when the pull of gravity was reduced, they may have flown outward into their long, narrow orbits. There is also a theory that at least some comets are long-distance space wanderers, coming into our solar system from interstellar space and traveling on again after moving past our sun.

Some of these theories are based on the way different comets behave. Today we know that most comets are repeat visitors to the space around our earth, although their visits may range from once every nine months to once in thousands of years. The frequency of their visits depends on the shape of the orbit in which they travel.

Like planets, comets trace huge elliptical trails around the sun. At their *perihelion* (the point when they are closest to the sun), some come very close indeed. In 1843, a comet came as close as 538,000 miles. Others keep their distance even at their nearest point of approach. The Comet of 1729 was nearly 383 million miles away from the sun at its perihelion. Imagine the size of that orbit! At *aphelion* (the point of an orbit farthest from the sun), comets can be incredibly far away. The Comet of 1844 was 406 *billion* miles away from the sun at aphelion. No wonder it takes some comets thousands of years to return.

The orbits of comets and the speed at which they travel can be affected jointly by the sun and by some of the planets. Fast comets plunging toward the sun may be deflected (pushed away) by Jupiter or Saturn into a hyperbolic orbit, which will cause the comet to move out of our solar system, never to return. Slow comets may be speeded into parabolic orbits when they are affected by the gravitational pull of the sun, while parabolic comets may be slowed into ellipses (Fig. 13). The massive planet Jupiter, with its strong gravitational force, may in fact sometimes "capture" wandering stray comets so that they become permanent members of our solar system.

The sun certainly attracts comets the way a burning flame attracts moths. As a comet gets closer, it becomes active, for its frozen gasses are released and its particles are spread out. Much of its substance is wasted, and while its tail grows in length as sunlight and the solar wind force the particles backward, the nucleus and the coma shrink.

By the time a comet becomes visible to the naked eye, it has usually been affected by the heat of the sun. Relatively few comets are visible without instruments. Most are telescopic comets, because they are invisible to the naked eye when they get near the sun.

Aside from the sun, the heavenly body that exerts the greatest influence on comets in our solar system may be the planet Jupiter. It is believed that Jupiter has a strong effect on the orbits of comets that stray too near. It is also possible that

The shape of a comet's orbit determines whether it will return to the vicinity of earth and what the time interval between visits will be.

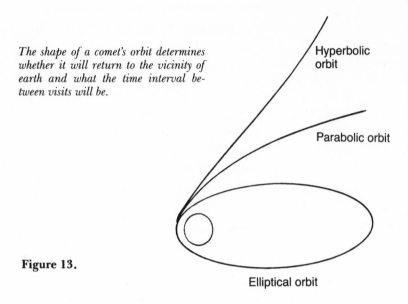

Figure 13.

other influences from outside our solar system may affect comets that travel close to the edge. Some "lost" comets may have been pulled into outer space.

Comets that are visible to the naked eye often linger above earth for long periods of time. Some stay around for years— which may have helped some earlier astronomers learn more about their behavior. Comets are identified by their orbits. And some have been rediscovered many times. Until the middle of the seventeenth century, each time a comet was sighted it was believed to be a new and unique visitor to earth. But in 1682, the English astronomer Edmund Halley predicted that the comet he was studying would return in 1758. Halley died in 1741, but his prediction proved true. Halley's Comet returned on schedule and has returned every seventy-six or seventy-seven years since then. Since Halley's time, many periodic comets have been identified and tagged with the names of their discoverers. Some of the better-known comets, besides Halley's, are Encke's, Biela's, Donati's, and Kohoutek's. Of course there are also many, many others. Biela's Comet broke into two parts in 1846 and then returned in a double form in 1852. Shortly afterward, it disappeared completely and does not return anymore. Perhaps, like other disintegrating comets, it broke up

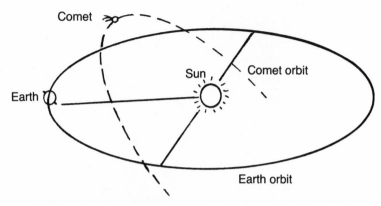

Figure 14. The relationship between the orbit of a comet and the path of the earth around the sun

into shoals of meteors. Some comets traveling along the same path may also be fragments of a larger comet that had broken up along the way.

Halley's Comet, with its dependable orbit and predictable cycle, is probably one of the most famous and most studied comets in the skies. We now know that Halley's Comet was responsible for many of the comet scares and sightings reported throughout history. And many of the comet stories told in the previous chapter were caused by one of this comet's frequent visits. On the basis of these old superstitions, one might say that Halley's Comet was responsible for a large share of the world's greatest disasters and wars!

Along with others, Halley's Comet has enabled scientists to learn much about the composition of our solar system and perhaps of the entire universe. Because comets that spend much of their time far away from the sun are less eroded and less changed than the planets and their satellites, they may give valuable clues to the origins of the universe. There are still many unanswered questions. For example, some scientists wonder if comets were responsible for bringing gases and organic materials to our lifeless, airless planet about four billion years ago. Did primitive living cells originate in comets and then "seed"

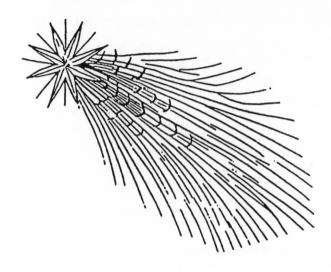

The comet of 1682 helped Edmund Halley to identify the seventy-six to seventy-seven-year cycle of that particular cyclical comet. Here it is as represented in the *Nuremburg Chronicles*.

the earth with life? Can comets be used as valuable models to study the original mix of minerals and gases from which life on earth arose?

What comets actually contain within their dust, ice, and gravel composition is a thin sprinkling of carbon, sulfur, and nitrogen, plus lots of water with a dusting of graphite, magnetite, and silicates. This may be very similar to the "primordial soup" found on our planet before life and before the formation of our atmosphere.

There are many other theories and questions about comets. One concerns the extinction of the world's dinosaurs and other species about sixty-five million years ago. Some have blamed this on the impact of a major comet. The huge dust cloud raised by the collision of a comet with earth could have obscured the sun for years, stunting plant growth and decreasing food supplies. Recently, there has been renewed interest in this almost discarded idea.

One group of scientists is studying a possible companion star to the sun that crosses the outer edge of the solar system at

60

The latest journey of Halley's Comet among the orbits of the planets.
Previously seen near Earth in 1910, the comet was farthest away from the sun in 1948, when it was somewhere between the orbits of Neptune and Pluto.

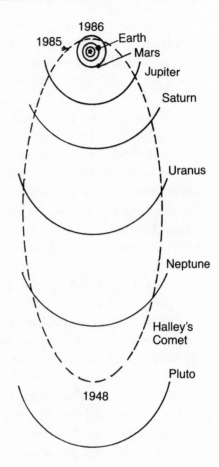

Figure 15.

intervals of about twenty-eight million years. In passing, this star, nicknamed Nemesis (after the Greek goddess of vengeance), disturbs the thick cloud of comets orbiting in that region and may well have sent some of them spinning out of orbit into the path of the earth. Nemesis came this way about sixty-five million years ago. Luckily, its next passage is not expected until fourteen million years from now.

A similar theory blames the sun itself for disturbing comet orbits periodically as the entire solar system travels through the Milky Way.

Although there is no real evidence of a comet collision with earth that may have brought about the extinction of the dinosaurs, there *is* evidence that a piece of a comet (in the form of a huge meteorite) might have crashed into a remote area of Siberia in 1908. The Siberian "comet" crater contains large quantities of the element irridium, which is normally not found in such quantities on earth.

Halley's Comet, on its return visit in 1985–1986, may answer some of the unresolved questions about the chemistry of comets and how it relates to that of other bodies in the solar system. Modern space technology makes a close-up study possible for the first time.

Astronomers expect to learn much about the composition of the dust in a comet, the types of frozen gas, the precise nature of the tail and coma. Comet studies include measurements of the changes in the comet's orbital position caused by the release of gas jets as the comet approaches the sun, and measurements of light at certain wavelengths. There are questions about the rate at which comets produce gas and dust. Photography provides the means to study the nucleus and tail formation, and spectroscopy helps identify new chemical compounds. Many of the techniques used to study comets have highly technical names, such as astronometry, radiometry, photometry, and polarimetry. By some of these methods, the size of dust particles can be measured and the amounts of solid material can be determined as the comet travels through starlight along its way.

For astronomers, the approach of Halley's Comet in 1985–1986 is a valuable and exciting event—an opportunity that will not recur until the year 2061. But on clear nights, this comet (which is ten times the size of Earth) offers a sky show even to comet buffs without telescopes and precision equipment. Reaching its perihelion (the position closest to the sun) on February 9, 1986, Halley's Comet comes closest to the earth on April 11, 1986, when its tail gradually becomes visible. The

In 1066, the appearance of Halley's Comet (before it was named, of course) was chronicled in a panel of the famous Bayeux tapestry, which hangs today in a fifteenth-century French cathedral. The comet was thought to foreshadow unpleasant events for King Harold of England.

best views of Halley's Comet are in the southern hemisphere, but it is visible for many weeks in the northern hemisphere, too—when viewed against a low and preferably uncluttered dark sky.

Watching Halley's Comet in 1986 gives us something in common with William the Conqueror, King Louis the Debonair, Increase Mather, Josephus, Julius Caesar, and possibly even Jesus in the year of his birth. And as we see the comet with our own eyes, we can understand the awe it produced in people of a less scientific age—people such as the poet Coleridge, who wrote:

Come and see! trust thine own eyes.
A fearful sign stands in the house of life;
An enemy: a fiend lurks close behind
the radiance of thy planet—oh! be warned!

63

Chapter 8

Meteors, Asteroids, and Assorted Space Debris

Newsweek columnist George F. Will once noted that if there were only three bees in the United States, the air would be more congested with bees than space is with stars. This tells us something about the vastness of space. Even though there are literally billions of objects floating about, ranging from the smallest particles of cosmic dust to the hugest of stars, the universe can apparently accommodate many billions more.

Even our own solar system is cluttered with all kinds of objects moving through and among the orbits of the charted planets and satellites. By one estimate, there may be about two hundred billion comets in the region halfway to the nearest star beyond Pluto's orbit and the sun. But the number of those space wanderers is dwarfed by the number of meteors and other bits and pieces of cosmic matter floating in that same area.

Meteors are fragments of matter hurtling through space at speeds up to twenty miles per second. They range in size from the tiniest dust particles to immense boulders. The name *meteor* comes from the Greek word *meteōros*, which means "raised and lofty." Normally meteors are not visible to the naked eye, but every day millions of them enter our atmosphere. And when they do, they create friction as their particles rub against air molecules, causing the temperature of those particles to rise by thousands of degrees. This, in turn, causes the bits of dust and gas to blaze up. The size, mass, and speed of the particle will determine the length and brightness of the visible streak of light.

Many meteors are formed when aging comets disintegrate, spilling the contents of their comas in their wake. For centuries after the death of a comet, such leftover particles continue to travel along in the same orbit once traversed by their parent comet. But while comets are visible and can be observed and paced over days and weeks, meteors flash by so quickly that they are gone in the blinking of an eye. That's why they are often called "shooting" or "falling" stars. While comets are usually regarded as the bearers of bad news, shooting stars have generally been greeted as happy omens. To many, those bright flashes of light in a dark sky seem like cheery greetings from outer space, and children are often told to wish on shooting stars.

Sometimes the flash of light produced by a burning meteor is so bright that it is even noticeable in daytime. Those meteors are generally called fireballs. Others actually explode, creating shock waves that produce a rumbling sound somewhat like thunder. Exploding meteors are called bolides.

People have noticed meteors since time immemorial—particularly the fireballs and bolides. In a document dating back to 687 B.C., the ancient Chinese spoke of stars that "fell like a shower." The Roman poet Virgil wrote in 30 B.C.:

Oft you shall see the stars, when wind is near
Shoot headlong from the sky,
And through the night
Leave in their wake
Long whitening seas of flame.

The Italian painter Raphael commemorated an especially bright fireball over the city of Milan in 1511 by painting the event into the background of one of his famous works, *The Ma-*

donna of Foligno. And a spectacular fireball explosion was reported over the city of Madrid on February 10, 1896. It is said that the fireball burst fourteen miles above the earth at 9:30 A.M. And though it was a clear and sunny morning, the explosion markedly brightened the day.

A bolide explosion, causing bright flashes of light and thunderlike rumblings when the sky is clear and blue, may have given rise to the expression "a bolt from the blue." Before people understood the nature of meteors, such an occurrence must have been a puzzling event.

Sometimes there are "showers" of shooting stars visible over a period of several hours or several nights. This happens when the earth moves through the path of a swarm of meteors from a disintegrating comet. A number of these meteor showers recur at the same time each year or at other regular cycles. The most predictable is the Perseid Meteor Shower, which returns annually during the first week of August.

The Perseid Meteor Shower is probably composed of particles spilled into space by a comet called Swift-Tuttle, which is slowly returning toward our sun. Swift-Tuttle comes close to earth only once every two hundred years. No one is sure whether the comet will return again or whether it has broken up completely in outer space. The trail of particles that it left behind, however, has been captured by the sun's gravity into an annual orbit.

The Perseid Shower got its name because its tiny streaks of bright light seem to come from or move toward the constellation named after the ancient Greek hero Perseus. (The Greeks named many of the groupings of stars they observed, and we continue to use these names today.) At peak moments of a Perseid Shower, as many as sixty or seventy fragments may blaze in one hour. The average Perseid fragment isn't much larger than a pea, and many are much smaller, but because it travels so swiftly, it burns brightly enough to be seen with the naked eye as it plunges through our atmosphere.

The Perseid Shower, which at one time was also known by the name St. Lawrence's Tears (because it appeared on the feast day of that saint), is only one of a number of familiar meteor showers. The Geminid Shower, visible in December, is another. Other regular meteor showers are thought to be related to Biela's and Halley's Comets.

Unfortunately, even though a great many meteors flare up in our atmosphere every year, spotting a shooting star or a shower of them is still a rare event. Flaming meteors can be seen best at night when the skies are clear and perfectly dark. When conditions are right, the patient sky watcher is rewarded by a dazzling display of bright flashing streaks that outshine the brightest stars.

Most meteor fragments vaporize into microscopic dust long before they come close to earth. Few come closer than about fifty-five miles above the earth's surface. The microscopic dust eventually travels down to earth, however, adding about one thousand tons per day to the mass of the earth.

Not all meteors are related to comets. Some come into being as a result of collisions between one or more asteroids. Most asteroids are oblong bits of matter—none of them larger than fifty or sixty miles across—in orbit between the orbits of Mars and Jupiter. These "little worlds" travel in a dense belt so closely packed together that collisions are almost inevitable. As the astronomer Carl Sagan wrote in his book *Cosmos*, "The asteroid belt is a great grinding mill, producing smaller pieces down to motes of dust."

Anyone who has ever read Antoine de Saint-Exupéry's *The Little Prince* knows, of course, that the tiny extraterrestrial being of that story came from Asteroid # B-612—a miniature world populated by a baobab tree, a few rosebushes, and of course the little prince himself. It's a lovely story, but real asteroids boast neither soil nor flowers nor any living things. They are barren, sterile bits of rock and iron, dating back to the beginnings of the solar system.

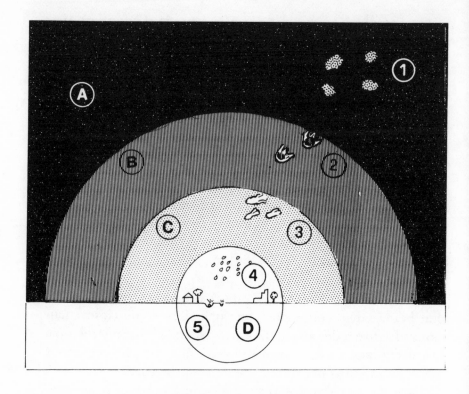

A. Outer Space
B. Upper atmosphere
C. Denser atmosphere
D. Earth

1. Invisible meteors
2. Meteors begin to glow
3. Burning Meteors
4. Meteors break up before reaching earth
5. Meteorites in impact craters

Figure 16. On their way through ever-denser layers of atmosphere, meteors burn and break up before some reach the ground.

The Journey of Meteors

Interstellar space: *Fragments of exploded stars (also called novae or "shooting stars") and other space debris may travel toward and sometimes into our solar system.*

Outer solar system: *Swarms of asteroids, exploded planets, and comets travel among and through the orbits of the planets.*

Outer atmosphere: *Broken pieces of matter enter the outer atmosphere as comets and are sometimes captured into orbit by the sun.*

Aging comets break up to form meteors. Novae break up into meteors. Friction causes meteors to glow and become visible.

Inner atmosphere: *Denser layers of atmosphere cause meteors to burn brightly. Some burn up completely before plunging to earth.*

Earth: *Unburned meteor fragments fall to earth in the form of meteorites. Most are tiny and remain on the surface as small pebbles. Larger ones will cause impact craters of varying depths and sizes.*

Finally, there are still other meteors that may have entered our own solar system from other parts of the galaxy or even from other galaxies. Some meteors now in orbit around the sun may date back to the beginnings of the universe itself and may contain material from interstellar space. Scientists can learn much about the earliest development of the earth and the solar system by examining fragments that have been affected by energy particles from the sun when it was billions of years younger.

Occasionally, chunks of meteor material do not burn up on their way through the atmosphere. When that happens, they hit the earth with such force that they sometimes create deep holes. Meteor chunks that reach the earth without burning up are called meteorites. Even small meteorites can furnish valuable information to scientists studying the history and composition of the universe. Some meteorites are composed mainly of stony material. Others are rich in minerals and ores. Breaking down materials in a meteorite can tell scientists about the age of the fragment and where it traveled in outer space.

There are many stories about incidents when even small meteorites came crashing through roofs into houses, often narrowly missing their occupants. Larger meteorites cause more serious damage.

Perhaps the most famous one that crashed to earth in modern times fell in 1908 into a forest in northern Siberia. The shock waves from its impact could be felt fifty miles away, and the bright flash was seen in full daylight for hundreds of miles. Luckily, the huge chunk, which weighed hundreds of tons, fell in an uninhabited area, where it scorched the earth and flattened trees in a circle more than twenty miles across. Another large meteorite exploded in the air above Siberia in 1947, peppering a mountainside with hundreds of crater holes.

There is evidence that other large meteorites have crashed into the earth in the remote past. The famous Meteor Crater in Arizona was probably created by the impact of an enormous meteorite somewhere between fifteen thousand and forty thousand years ago. The huge hole is more than 4,000 feet wide and 570 feet deep. As the meteorite burrowed into the earth, it threw up a wall of earth around its perimeter more than 150 feet above ground level. The meteorite itself shattered on impact. Scientists believe that the energy released by its impact may have resembled that of a four-megaton nuclear explosion. Any living things unlucky enough to be in the vicinity surely didn't live to tell the tale!

Just as there are tales about collisions with comets in the distant past, so are there theories that the collision of a huge meteorite or asteroid with Earth contributed to the extinction of the dinosaurs, for the same reasons described in Chapter 6.

There are large meteorite craters dating back to prehistoric times scattered around the United States, Canada, and other parts of the world, but they are relatively few in number and were created over a period of many millions of years. Luckily, the chances of Earth receiving more major meteorite "wounds" in the foreseeable future is minimal—thanks to the layer of atmosphere that has formed a protective mantle around our

This drawing, titled "Shooting Stars," actually shows the meteor shower of November 12, 1799. This might have been either the Leonids Shower, which occurs regularly around that time or the Andromedids (which may be fragments of Biela's comet).

planet for the last four billion years or so. Our atmosphere, which makes life possible on this little planet, shields us effectively from constant bombardment by space debris. We only need to look at pictures of the moon or of Mercury—whose surfaces are pockmarked by meteor craters—to recognize how lucky we really are.

While the biggest meteorites that made it down to the surface of the earth have usually shattered completely on impact, a few sizable chunks have been found. The largest, weighing about sixty-six tons, was found in West Africa. Another, weighing about thirty-four tons, was found in Greenland. The largest meteorite ever seen to fall in historical times came down on November 16, 1492, in Ensisheim, France. It weighed 280 pounds.

Sightings of small meteorites falling through the sky date back thousands of years. In early times people believed that such stones were sent by the gods. Beads made from metal-containing meteorites have been found in ancient graves in Egypt and Babylonia. Scholars know that the source of those beads were meteorites, because the beads contained nickel and iron long before iron mining and smelting were known.

The ancient Greeks were the first to recognize that meteorites contained iron. In fact, their word for iron was sidēros to indicate that this metal was sidereal, meaning "from the stars." Even today the word siderite is often used for iron-bearing meteorites, while stony meteorites are sometimes called *aerolites* or *uranolites*.

The fall of a meteorite over a town in France in 1492. Fragments of this meteorite still survive today.

Because people believed that these stones from the sky were sent by the gods, some meteorites were treated with reverence. It is thought that the Kaaba, the black sacred stone in the Islamic holy shrine at Mecca in Saudi Arabia, may be a meteorite.

At the beginning of the scientific age, when people began to understand the workings of the solar system, doubts crept in about the source of those falling stones. Many argued that there was nothing in the solar system besides the known planets and moons. Finally, a particularly heavy fall of meteorites in France in 1804 convinced some of those skeptics that there was such a thing as stones from the skies. More than two thousand stones fell on the town of L'Aigle that day, to the dismay of its inhabitants.

Once scientists began to accept the fact that meteorites were indeed fragments of shattered asteroids and bits of material that had traveled a vast distance in outer space, they were able to learn a great deal from these tiny space intruders about the history and composition of the universe. For many centuries, meteorites provided the only concrete answers to questions about cosmic history.

Today, spacecraft landing on the moon, Mars, and other planets have brought back the kind of information once available only from meteorites crashing randomly into Earth. At the same time, the growing number of space vehicles orbiting Earth and traveling beyond our solar system is adding a new dimension to visual sightings in the skies. At certain times and places, when the skies are clear and city lights do not obscure our vision, orbiting spacecraft can be seen with the naked eye as bright moving lights above the horizon.

So when we see lights moving across our night skies, what do we think in this modern day and age? Is it an airplane, a satellite, a shooting star? Or is it something strange and sinister—an alien presence in our midst?

Somehow we are loath to give up superstitions. Almost no one speaks of omens and messages from the gods anymore when they see lights in the skies they can't identify. Most people know about eclipses and meteors and comets. And yet, like our ancestors who thought they saw fiery dragons, hairy monsters, and flaming swords in the heavens above them, some people still try to see alien objects in the dark shadows behind bright moving lights in the skies. In our modern scientific age, these fancies take the form of "flying saucers" and other assorted unidentified flying objects (UFO's). It makes no difference that most of these odd sightings can eventually be identified as low-flying planes or space capsules or weather balloons. Not *all* of them have been explained, and so there is room for speculation.

The spaces that surround our little earth are vast, mysterious, and still largely unexplored even in these days of space travel, radio telescopes, and other sophisticated instruments and machines. We still know so little about what is out there beyond our solar system, beyond our galaxy. While many of the spectacular "sky shows" happen at predictable intervals, there are always surprises. No one can tell how many pieces of cosmic debris will make their way into our solar system, how many will be captured by the gravitational pull of our sun. Nor are any two eclipses ever exactly the same, either in appearance or duration.

We don't need to attach supernatural or extraterrestrial meanings to the unusual happenings in our skies. Their predictable recurrence is a small miracle in itself. When we watch eclipses and cyclical comets, we relive events experienced by our remotest ancestors and their descendants through the centuries. There is a reassurance in the constancy of these heavenly movements. We are at our appointed place in the scheme of the universe, and the pattern of stars and planets and wandering objects in space serves to remind us that no matter what we do, our earth is part of a larger system that has operated predictably since the beginning of time.

Appendix 1:
Eclipse Schedule,
1985–2010

TOTAL AND ANNULAR TOTAL ECLIPSES

Year	Date	Dura-tion (min.: sec.)	Location
1985	Nov.12	1:59	Antarctica
1986	Oct. 3*	0:01	N. Atlantic Ocean
1987	Mar.29*	0:08	S. Atlantic Ocean, Africa
1988	Mar.18	3:46	Indonesia, Philippines
1991	Jul.11	6:54	Hawaii, Mexico, S. America
1992	Jun.30	5:20	S. Atlantic Ocean
1994	Nov. 3	4:23	S. America, S. Atlantic Ocean
1995	Oct.24	2:10	India, Southeast Asia, Indonesia
1997	Mar. 9	2:50	Arctic Ocean, Russia
1998	Feb.26	4:08	Pacific Ocean, Venezuela, Atlantic Ocean
1999	Aug.11	2:23	Europe, Middle East, India
2001	Jun.21	4:56	S. Atlantic Ocean, S. Africa
2002	Dec. 4	2:04	S. Africa, Australia
2003	Nov.23	1:57	Antarctica
2005	Apr. 8*	0:42	S. Pacific Ocean
2006	Mar.29	4:05	S. America, Africa, Asia
2008	Aug. 1	2:27	Canada, Greenland, China
2009	Jul.22	6:39	Southeast Asia, Pacific Ocean
2010	Jul.11	5:20	Argentina, Chile, Pacific Ocean

Appendix 2:
Chart of Eclipse Paths,
1985–2010

**TOTAL SOLAR ECLIPSES AND
ANNULAR TOTAL ECLIPSES**

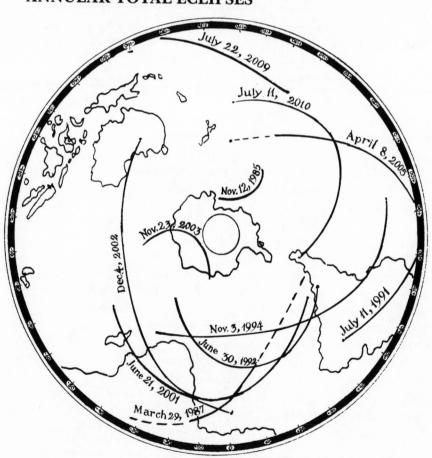

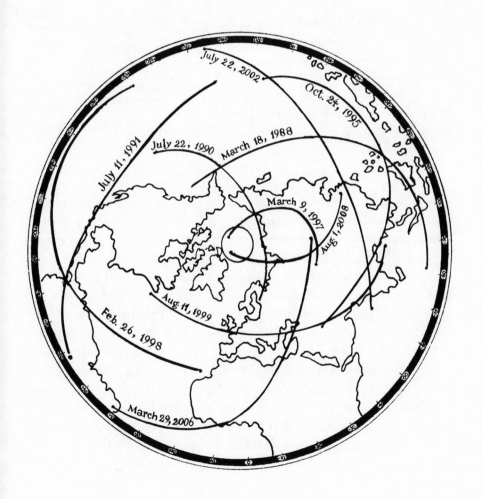

Appendix 3:
Two More Safe Ways
to View Eclipses

NEVER look at an eclipse directly—
not even with sunglasses or smoked lenses!

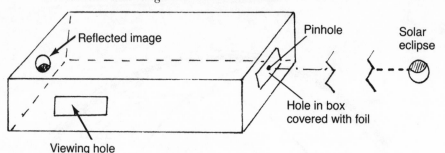

PINHOLE PROJECTOR

One must never look directly at the sun when watching an eclipse, because some of the infrared and ultraviolet rays of the sun can permanently damage the retina of the eyes or even cause blindness. It is particularly dangerous to look at the sun through a telescope or with binoculars. Even sunglasses or smoked lenses do not offer sufficient protection. The safest way to view an eclipse is to project the image of the sun onto a white surface on the ground, using a piece of cardboard with a pinhole, or by making a simple *pinhole projector* (see illustrations).

It is possible to watch the total phase of an eclipse safely through viewers made from two layers (60 density) of doubly exposed black and white film (so that the film is very black) since the metal in the layers of exposed film protects the eye from the ultraviolet rays. But this is safe only when the film has been properly prepared!

78

1. *With the sun at your back, reflect the sun through a pinhole in a piece of cardboard onto another piece of white cardboard.*

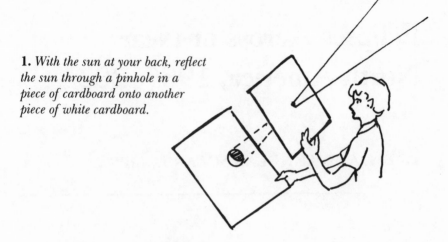

2. *Also with the sun behind you, capture its image through a telescope or binoculars pointing downward to a piece of white paper on the ground. (Do not look through the telescope!)*

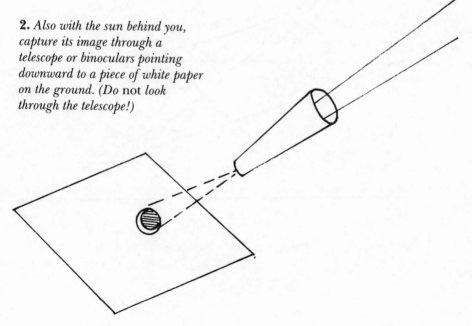

Appendix 4:
Eclipses Across or Near
North America, 1985–2023

TOTAL AND ANNULAR SOLAR ECLIPSES

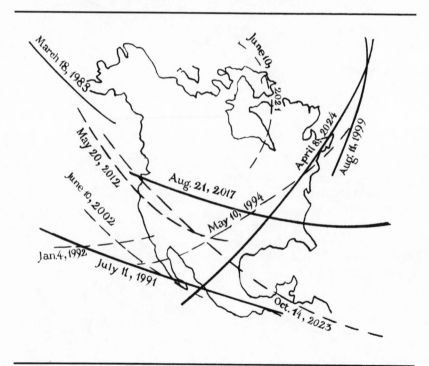

Appendix 5:
Periodic Comets

SOME RECENT VISITORS,
BOTH SHORT-TERM AND LONG-TERM

Name of Comet	Years (return to perihelion)
Encke	3.30
Grigg-Skjellerup	4.91
Tuttle-Giacobini-Kresak	5.48
Tuttle	13.61
Halley	76.04
Grigg-Mellish	164.30
Mrkos (1957)	12,800
Humason (1962)	2,900
Alcock (1963)	15,400
Barbon (1966)	34,000
Ikeya-Seki (1968)	89,000
Tago-Sato-Kosaka (1969)	419,000

Note: Comets are named after the people who identified them first.

Appendix 6:
Major Meteor Showers

Quadrantanids	Jan. 1–5
Lyrids	Apr. 19–24
Aquarids-Eta	May 1–4
Aquarids-Delta	July 15–Aug. 15
Perseids	July 24–Aug. 18
Orionids	Oct. 16–26
Taurids	Oct. 20
Leonids	Nov. 16–?
Geminids	Dec. 7–15
Ursids	Dec. 17–24

Note: Meteor showers are the remnants of a disintegrating comet moving along the orbit of the original comet. They are named after the constellations from which they seem to originate.

Glossary

Aerolites   Stony meteorite fragments.

Annular Eclipse   A solar eclipse during which the shadow of the moon does not fully cover the sun, so that a narrow ring of light is visible at the edges.

Aphelion   The point of an orbit farthest away from the sun.

Asteroids   Minor planets, most of them less than fifty or sixty miles in diameter and in orbit between the orbits of Mars and Jupiter.

Astronometry   A method to measure the changes of a comet's position in orbit.

Astrophysicist   An astronomer who studies the physical nature of heavenly bodies, such as their chemistry, temperature, light, and origin.

Atmosphere   Several layers of gases, dust, and moisture that surround the earth.

Baily's Beads   Ragged points of sunlight visible around the edges of a total eclipse that are caused by some of the high mountains on the surface of the moon.

Bolides   Exploding fireballs (extremely bright meteors which may produce a thunderlike noise as they explode).

Chromosphere ("Ball of color")   A gaseous layer just above the edge of the solar disk.

Coma   A halo of gases surrounding the nucleus of a comet.

Comet   A collection of gravel, dust, and minerals surrounded by a cloudlike mass of gases. May be a remnant of an exploded planet or leftover space debris.

Comet Head   The nucleus of a comet with its surrounding halo of gases (coma).

Comet Nucleus   A loose collection of gravel, dust, and minerals at the center of a comet.

Comet Tail   A mixture of dust and gases that is blown backward from the comet's head by the heat of the sun and by solar winds.

Constellation   A group of stars forming a visible pattern in the sky.

Corona The upper layer of gases surrounding the main body of the sun.

Cyclical Comets Comets that return to the vicinity of earth at regular, predictable intervals, ranging from three to eighty years.

Earthshine Sunlight reflected by the earth to the moon.

Eclipse An eclipse occurs when one heavenly body is hidden by the shadow of another.

Ecliptic The seeming path of the sun through the sky.

Ellipses The oval-shaped paths traced by various heavenly bodies around the sun or around each other.

Fireballs A brightly burning meteor that produces a flash so bright that it is visible even in daylight.

Flying Saucer A nickname for unidentified flying objects (also known as UFO's).

Galaxy A large system of stars, dust, and gas held together by the force of gravity.

Gravitational Field The curvature around a massive body in space that forces smaller bodies into orbits around the larger body.

Halley, Edmund An English astronomer (1656–1742) who recognized that certain different comet sightings were due to the periodic return of the same comet, which was hence named Halley's comet.

Helmet Streamers Flaming masses of gas flaring upward from the chromosphere (the layer just above the main body of the sun) into the lower corona.

Hyperbolic Orbit An open-ended orbit that causes some comets to pass through the solar system once, never to return again. (See figure 13.)

Interstellar Space The vast space beyond the solar system stretching between the billions of galaxies and stars in the universe.

Lunar Eclipse A lunar eclipse occurs when the earth comes between the sun and the moon and its shadow prevents sunlight from striking the moon, seemingly blotting it out.

Meteor A particle or chunk of matter traveling through the earth's atmosphere. When meteors are heated by friction with the atmosphere, they glow and become visible.

Meteor Shower A swarm of meteors that occurs when the earth passes through the orbit of a disintegrating comet.

Meteorite A piece of assorted space debris—often from a disintegrating comet, but occasionally material originating in the interstellar spaces—called a meteor in space; a meteorite once it falls to earth.

Meteorite Crater A depression in the surface of a planet caused by the impact of a meteorite.

Milky Way The galaxy (system of stars, planets, and dust) that contains our own solar system.

Nebular Disk A thick cloud of gas and dust found within a galaxy.

Nodes The two points where the moon is in or near the plane of the earth's orbit around the sun. At those points, eclipses can occur.

Orbit The path traced by a heavenly object around the sun or a planet.

Parabolic Orbit A widely curved path traveled by some occasionally returning comets. (See figure 13.)

Partial Eclipse An eclipse in which the sun is only partially hidden by the shadow of the moon.

Penumbra The half-shadow cone cast on the earth beyond the path of a total eclipse and during partial and annular eclipses.

Perihelion The point of an orbit closest to the sun.

Periodic Comet A comet that returns to the vicinity of the earth at various but often infrequent intervals. Return visits may range from three or four years to thousands of years.

Phase A particular moment in a changing series of appearances of a heavenly body. In the case of the moon, for instance, increasing and decreasing "slices" of moon visible during the course of a month reflect different phases.

Photometry A method of studying light at varying wavelengths.

Photosphere ("Ball of light") The luminous solar disk as it appears to the naked eye.

Polar Plumes Tall solar flares that soar upward from the sun's polar regions into the corona.

Polarimetry A method of studying the vibrations of light beams.

Primordial Soup The mixture of gases and minerals presumed to have existed in the waters of this planet in the millennia before life originated.

Prominences Tall luminous clouds of gas thrusting upward from the sun's surface into the corona.

Radiometry A method used to study the intensity of energy, applied in comet studies to explore the chemistry of heavenly bodies.

Saros Cycle The cycle of eclipses recurring every eighteen years as charted by the ancient Babylonians and confirmed by modern science.

Satellite A heavenly body traveling in orbit around another. Today the word is often used for man-made objects, such as space capsules.

Shadow Bands Wavering light patterns cast on the earth just before a solar eclipse reaches totality.

Siderite A word from the Greek, meaning "iron from the stars." Used for metal-bearing meteorites, this word shows an early recognition that these stones came from the sky.

Solar Eclipse When the moon travels in a direct line between the sun and the earth, its shadow seems to cover the disk of the sun during its passage.

Solar System The group of heavenly bodies including the star we call the sun, its nine planets, and other satellites.

Solar Wind Electrically charged particles streaming out from the sun at vast speeds and reaching millions of miles into space.

Spectroscope A tool used to identify the speed and direction of an object in space by studying its band of colors.

Telescopic Comet   A comet so far away from earth that it can be seen only with the help of a telescope.

UFO   Unidentified Flying Object, believed by some to be extraterrestrial spaceships. Most UFO's are probably asteroids, meteorites, novae (shooting stars), or reflected lights.

Umbra   The deep shadow cast by one heavenly body on the surface of another during an eclipse.

Universe   The infinite system of stars, planets, and galaxies sometimes called the cosmos.

Uranolites   Another name for stony meteorites.

Bibliography

Astronomical Myths, by John T. Blake. London: McMillan, 1877.

Astronomy for Amateurs, by Camille Flammarion. New York: Appleton, 1910.

Astronomy of the Ancients, ed. by Kenneth Brecher and Michael Feirtag. Cambridge, Mass.: MIT Press, 1979.

Astronomy with Binoculars, by James Muirden. New York: Crowell, 1979.

Cambridge Encyclopedia of Astronomy, ed. by Simon Milton. New York: Crown, 1977.

Canon of Eclipses, by Theodore R. von Oppolzer. New York: Dover Publications, 1962.

Canon of Solar Eclipses, by J. Grosjean Meeus and W. Vanderleen. Oxford, Eng.: Pergamon Press, 1966.

The Case for the UFO, by M. K. Jessup. Jane Lew, W. Va.: Barker Books, 1973.

The Comet Is Coming! The Feverish Legacy of Mr. Halley, by Nigel Calder. New York: Viking, 1981.

Comet Lore, by Edwin Emerson. Schilling Press, 1910.

Comets, Meteors, and Men, by Peter Lancaster Brown. New York: Taplinger, 1974.

Corona and Coronet: An Eclipse Journey to Japan, by Mable Todd. Boston: Houghton Mifflin, 1898.

Cosmos, by Carl Sagan. New York: Random House, 1980.

An Eclipse Party in Africa, by Eban Loomis. Boston: Houghton Mifflin, 1898.

Eclipses, by Bryan Brewer. Seattle, Wash.: Earth View, 1978.

Eclipses of the Sun and Moon, by Frank Dyson and R. v. d. R. Woolley. Oxford, Eng.: Clarendon Press, 1937.

The First Stargazers: An Introduction to the Origins of Astronomy, by James Cornell. New York: Scribner, 1981.

Man and the Stars, by Hanbury Brown. New York: Oxford University Press, 1978.

Myths and Marvels of Astronomy, by Richard A. Proctor. New York: Putnam, 1877.

Orbiting the Sun: Planets and Satellites of the Solar System, by Fred L. Whipple. Cambridge, Mass.: Harvard University Press, 1981.

The Picture History of Astronomy, by Patrick Moore. Grosset, 1961.

Popular Astronomy, by Camille Flammarion. New York: Appleton, N.D.

The Romance of Comets, by Mary Proctor. New York: Harper & Brothers, 1926.

Stonehenge Decoded, by Gerald Hawkins and John B. White. New York: Dell, 1966.

Stonehenge of the Kings, by Patrick Crampton. New York: John Day, 1967.

The Story of Comets, by George F. Chambers. Oxford, Eng.: Clarendon Press, 1909.

The Story of Eclipses, by George F. Chambers. Philadelphia: Ridgeway, 1904.

Teaching a Stone to Talk, by Annie Dillard. New York: Harper & Row, 1982.

Tripolis the Mysterious, by Mable Todd. Small Maynard, 1912.

The Universe: Its Beginning and End, by Lloyd Motz. New York: Scribner, 1976.

Watchers of the Skies, by Willy Ley. New York: Viking, 1963.

Index